A School in Trouble

A Personal Story of Central Falls High School

William R. Holland

ROWMAN & LITTLEFIELD EDUCATION
A division of
ROWMAN & LITTLEFIELD PUBLISHERS, INC.
Lanham • New York • Toronto • Plymouth, UK

Published by Rowman & Littlefield Education
A division of Rowman & Littlefield Publishers, Inc.
A wholly owned subsidiary of
The Rowman & Littlefield Publishing Group, Inc.
4501 Forbes Boulevard, Suite 200, Lanham, Maryland 20706
http://www.rowmaneducation.com

Estover Road, Plymouth PL6 7PY, United Kingdom

British Library Cataloguing in Publication Information Available

Library of Congress Cataloging-in-Publication Data

Holland, William R., 1938–
  A school in trouble : a personal story of Central Falls High School /
William R. Holland.
      p. cm.
  Includes bibliographical references.
  ISBN 978-1-60709-873-7 (cloth : alk. paper) — ISBN 978-1-60709-874-4
(pbk. : alk. paper) — ISBN 978-1-60709-875-1 (ebook)
  1. Central Falls High School (Central Falls, R.I.). 2. Hispanic
Americans—Education (Secondary)—Rhode Island—Central Falls. I. Title.
  LD7501.C2827H65 2010
  373'.97451—dc22   2010013970

∞ ™ The paper used in this publication meets the minimum requirements
of American National Standard for Information Sciences—Permanence of
Paper for Printed Library Materials, ANSI/NISO Z39.48-1992.

Printed in the United States of America

Contents

Foreword

"We must accept finite disappointment, but we must never lose infinite hope."

—Dr. Martin Luther King Jr.

Those profound words, although spoken decades ago, hold true today. We are constantly disappointed, in one way or another, in what we encounter in our communities, schools, and even families. But we should never lose hope—that would be the ultimate failure and disappointment.

Central Falls High School has been thrust into a national movement and debate over the future of public education. All eyes are on the tiniest city in the smallest state in America.

The community of Central Falls is made up of hardworking, mostly immigrant, and poor families whose children's futures depend almost entirely on the quality of their education. For them, the stakes are high. For them, there is no room for error. For them, mediocrity is a life sentence to the underclass, where poverty and disenfranchisement have flourished for generations.

In my work as the chair of the Central Falls School Board of Trustees over the past four years, I have encountered many pockets of hope. I hear about the dreams of young people who are thirsty for excellence and hungry for opportunities.

I see parents who want their children to have a better life than they did. I encounter professionals and educators who have high expectations for themselves and for their students. I see generous individuals who freely give their time and resources.

I also see students graduate and go on to pursue their dreams, perhaps the first member of their family to graduate high school and go to college. I witness miracles when I see young special-needs children struggle to read and write and be just like any other child in the classroom.

I am enveloped with culture and diversity from every corner. I am saturated by history and by the legacies of pioneers who came before me. This all gives me tremendous hope.

However, I also encounter cynicism, racism, low expectations, and apathy. I stare at the powerful status quo. I witness the needs of children bought and sold as in a common marketplace. I feel the deafening silence of the many young people who don't survive the barren desert that is school.

I cringe at the blaming, the excuses, the looking the other way, the "these kids can't" anthem ringing in my ears. It is easy to lose hope when bombarded with failure and neglect.

When I first arrived at Central Falls, I was wide-eyed and convinced that the road of public service I had chosen was going to be fulfilling and important. Well, I was right. It has been a passion and a quest that I can't stop. Why? Because what I have encountered was so deeply disturbing that it moved my conscience and my soul. The failure and struggle in the school district was overwhelming—even for me, a native of Central Falls.

The community has changed, but the schools have not. I often come home after board meetings with a dumbfounded expression on my face, and my husband asks me how the meeting went. When I share my concerns and observations, he shakes his head and says, "That sounds like when I was a student at Central Falls High School." And that was more than twenty years ago! So many years have passed, and yet it is as if time stands still in our high school.

Along with my fellow trustees and superintendent, Dr. Fran Gallo, we refuse to preserve the status quo. We have embarked on a journey that has the potential to bring Central Falls High School from worst to first in Rhode Island. It is difficult and thankless work, but I can't think of a better legacy than to empower a new generation of children to become whatever they want to be.

Providing the kind of real reform that students deserve will change their lives forever. I know how powerful that is. I see the value that a good education has had for me and my family. I am the middle class. I am the new face of America, and I refuse to enjoy my privileges and power without reaching out to ensure that the children of Central Falls will follow.

In Bill Holland's book *A School in Trouble: A Personal Story of Central Falls High School*, he speaks about hope, challenges, and self-inflicted impediments that keep meaningful education reform out of reach. His work is a snapshot of the good, the bad, and the incredible.

Although we may not have all the answers and often aren't even sure what real change and reform look and feel like, we can believe that if we have hope, we can do almost anything! It is hard to explain, but that is exactly what sustains this important movement in Central Falls.

—Anna Cano Morales
Chair, Central Falls School Board of Trustees

Acknowledgments

My heartfelt thanks go to the four students and families profiled in this book. The students are wonderful people and gave freely of their time during their demanding freshman year in college. Thanks also go to Central Falls teachers Ron Thompson, Bob Scappini, Doris White, and Kathy Casalino, who provided invaluable insight into what made the four students so special. I did not select them; they were identified by students as teachers who made a difference in the school and their personal lives.

Special thanks go to teachers Deloris Grant and Josh LaPlante, who took extra time to provide me with extensive commentary and knowledgeable perspectives on the challenges, joys, and personal fulfillment of teaching underprivileged students in an urban high school.

Further gratitude goes to Judy Robinson, who has served as my editor during the writing of my books. As a former high school English teacher, she has been instrumental in reminding me of the realities of teaching adolescents in high school. I thank her for keeping me grounded.

Finally, I want to thank all the members of the Central Falls school community for their past support and making me feel that I am still welcomed and valued as an educator.

Introduction

I am a former superintendent, college professor, and Rhode Island Commissioner of Higher Education who retired in July 2005 as professor emeritus at Rhode Island College in Providence and, like a few professional educators I knew, looked forward to writing my memoirs—thinking they may be of interest to someone, even if only to my children, grandchildren, and great grandchildren. However, one year later I accepted an interim position as superintendent of schools in Central Falls, Rhode Island, after the previous superintendent resigned that July.

Although I had been a superintendent in suburban school districts in Rhode Island and Massachusetts for nearly two decades, I hadn't been a superintendent for eighteen years. And although I had been a consultant, I had never actually been employed full time by an urban school district in any capacity.

The Central Falls school district was taken over by the state in 1991 because of declining local revenue and its inability to finance its schools. After a short period of direct control by the State Department of Education, a school board of trustees was appointed by and accountable to the commissioner and the state Board of Regents for Elementary and Secondary Education.

The regents are appointed by the governor and report directly to him. It should be noted that the governor has considerable influence over the regents, as does the Rhode Island State Legislature, since it has final approval of the district school budget.

In addition to serving as interim superintendent and being charged with organizing a search for his successor, I was expected to conduct a detailed study recommending major reform initiatives for a district suffering from chronically low student performance.

However, that fall I found that incremental progress was occurring in student achievement in the elementary schools and in the middle school due to the success of several new programs and targeted teacher training.

My reform recommendations were therefore focused on low-performing Central Falls High School, a school that resembled the ones referred to in UCLA's Civil Rights Project 2007 report as subpar "dropout factories."

The report called the large majority of children of color in inner-city schools examples of an increasing number of underprivileged minority students who are now more segregated than they had been since Martin Luther King Jr.'s death in 1968, underscoring the powerful relationship between segregation and dropout rates.

The UCLA findings also indicated that between 1968 and 2005 the percentage of white public school students fell from 80 percent to 57 percent, while the Latino enrollment nearly quadrupled—with that population being even more segregated than blacks. *Time* magazine, in fact, identified the growing problem as the most "underreported" story of 2009.

My choices for reform of the high school were to recommend reopening as a charter school, placing the school under State Department of Education management, restructuring staffing or governance, replacing all or most of the staff, or placing the school under private management.

Since the state legislature had placed a moratorium on approving new charter schools, that option was not available. Due to a myriad of legal obstacles relating to teacher certification and the fact that there were only nine hundred pupils in the high school, replacing or transferring all or most of the staff was not feasible. More significantly, the lack of sufficient, credible, evaluative data on teacher performance made it difficult in pro-union Rhode Island to discharge tenure teachers, who comprised 90 percent of the faculty.

I did replace two principals, transferred one principal and several teachers, and reassigned staff to new roles and responsibilities. However, my major recommendation was to dramatically restructure the high school by collaborating with the University of Rhode Island (URI), the state flagship university.

I wanted to infuse the school with additional and valuable human, social, and financial capital, the type that could help the school with sorely needed professional assistance, new ideas and services, and additional resources, especially increased private funding.

My recommendations for change, entitled "Critical Next Steps for the Central Falls School District," were formally accepted by the commissioner, the regents, and Governor Donald Carcieri in April 2007. The proposal called for major redesign of the high school, and the formation of the University of Rhode Island Academy at Central Falls High School.

It was designed as a comprehensive, five-year formal partnership that would provide Central Falls High School with university staff and new services and resources in order to support a turnaround of the chronically low-performing school.

Robert Carothers, URI president in 2007, enthusiastically supported the new initiative and provided his personal assistance in gaining state and college faculty approval and private funding.

Dr. Fran Gallo, former deputy superintendent in Providence who had successfully led secondary-school reform efforts in that city, succeeded me as superintendent in April 2007. With URI and faculty assistance, she immediately crafted a detailed restructuring plan that was initiated at the start of the 2007–2008 school year. Also playing a major role was Anna Cano Morales, chair of the Central Falls Board of Trustees, whose leadership, passion, and commitment to Latino families and students have been an inspiration to all.

The critical need to improve the educational attainment for Latino students in Central Falls and Rhode Island and narrow the gap in educational achievement between Latinos and whites parallels the national scene. There is a growing problem that is now a major crisis in our nation's high schools, as Latino students continue to fall behind their white counterparts with shockingly low graduation rates, poor literacy, and low college-preparedness rates; Latinos have the highest dropout rate of any race.

The problem must be addressed now since it is not going away. Similar to the UCLA findings, statistics published by the U.S. Department of Education indicate that five million Latino students were enrolled in America's public schools in 1994. By 2006, that number had doubled.

While the percentage of white students has declined and that of African American students has held steady, the number of Latino students has significantly increased. The median age of Latinos is also ten years younger than the rest of the nation's population and is clearly reflected in rising Latino birth rates.

This demographic reality commands immediate attention from educators, politicians, and all those who are vested in public education. The future economic and social well-being of Rhode Island and the rest of our country is at stake unless we can educate current and future generations of Latino students to high educational standards.

This book is therefore about a dedicated mission undertaken in 2007 by the Central Falls school district to reform its low-performing high school and to better educate its Latino students.

To illustrate the struggles and realities of being educated in an inner-city school district, the book focuses on four recent Central Falls High School graduates, class of 2009. Their compelling stories describe how they beat the odds and achieved school success in spite of personal adversity and other situational obstacles they had to overcome.

It is a behind-the-scenes look at the critical role parents, schools, and communities play in education, and provides valuable insight into what these entities must do if more Central Falls students are to join the four profiled graduates and realize brighter futures.

The book also illustrates the rocky road to urban school reform, as we see Central Falls High School navigate through the maze of federal and state laws and strong union opposition as it tries to achieve deep and sustainable change and improvement.

In December 2009, the school was notified that a new federal mandate had given the superintendent and state commissioner of education new authority to transform schools in the lowest five percent of "persistently low-performing schools" in the state. The mandate was quite stringent in its requirements and of course not available to me three years previously, when I made my recommendations for change.

A new commissioner protocol generated by the mandate required Central Falls High School to select one of four models for corrective action in 2010. They were: close the school and terminate the principal; increase learning time and change instruction; hire a charter school or an outside management company to run the school, in which case all current teachers would be terminated; terminate all teachers and administrators with the possibility of rehiring up to fifty percent of those terminated.

This new requirement created a firestorm within the district and pitted the superintendent, board of trustees, and state commissioner of education against the local and state AFT teachers' union in a hostile battle of wills.

CHAPTER 1

Interim Superintendent in Central Falls

"What was it like being an interim superintendent of schools in Central Falls? When I heard you had been appointed superintendent there, I laughed. How long had it been since you were a superintendent? About twenty years, right? You had been in those nice little white, affluent suburban districts and then escaped to that charmed life of a college professor. You really didn't know much about inner-city schools, old man, did you?"

It was September 2009, two and a half years after I had left the district after eight months as interim superintendent. I stared intently at my old colleague, whom I hadn't seen for years, pausing as I thought about how to respond to his sarcastic put-down.

"You know, John, it actually was the most fulfilling professional and personal experience in my forty-three years in public education. Truly transformational."

The way John stared at me I could tell he thought I was crazy. "You've got to be kidding! I read where you had to handle a sensitive racial incident and a bus driver union sickout, slash the budget you inherited by over two million dollars, and develop a plan to turn the failing high school around. And that's just for starters, right?"

Taken aback by his brash manner, I said, "Yes, those are just starters. But there's much more."

John wouldn't let up. "I hear you did all this with the State Department of Education in your face, establishing deadlines and demanding corrective action. That must have been fun."

Although he was right on target, John still wouldn't stop. He had much more to say.

"A former Central Falls principal told me the other day that the teachers' contract is worse than the one in Providence. The union files grievances if an administrator sneezes too much. They want so much for every sneeze over three a day."

John was getting ridiculous. It was time for me to set him straight once and for all. I got on my pulpit and started my sermon.

"It was definitely 24-7, and every day brought a new crisis of some nature. However, I learned an incredible amount about immigrant Latino families and their life struggles. I saw up close how poverty, low expectations, and other sociological and cultural differences contribute to school failure and broken dreams.

"I also learned that Latino families, a large number of whom are single-parent families headed by mothers—although reluctant and not knowing how to best do it—want their children to succeed in school and have successful futures just as badly as better-educated white, suburban parents do. But more importantly, I loved the parents and their kids."

John was incredulous. "What do you mean you loved the parents and the kids?"

"I loved their passion, their pride, and their joy and appreciation for the little things you did for their children. I loved the respect they had for us as educators and for what we were trying to do to improve the situation. You could see the appreciation in their eyes and their smiles. Just like the waves of past immigrants to our shores, they want their kids to have a better life than they have had. This sense of gratitude is definitely more in abundance in Central Falls than in suburban districts. It is also the reason that many dedicated and caring teachers spend their entire careers in Central Falls schools."

"But you know the reputation Central Falls has, don't you? Remember I had relatives that used to live here," John said.

"I do know, but it's obvious that you want to tell me, so go ahead."

"Well, first it's a city that still can't generate enough revenue to finance its schools. The state is spending over fifty million bucks a year and getting little in return. Gang wars, drug busts, domestic assaults and other crimes abound in a city where they had to institute a curfew last year after some teenage shootings.

"It is a city that continues to have low-performing schools with low graduation rates and high dropout rates. Its high school is doing so badly that it should be closed down."

"John, I know all that. You aren't telling me anything I don't know. But much of what you say is a bit exaggerated and overshadows some of the great things about this culturally rich and diverse city and its schools. All you know is what you read in the newspapers.

"For example, the elementary schools are succeeding with a greater number of students and have escaped from the low-performing classification. And state test scores only measure so much anyway. The schools are safe and students are courteous and respectful. The schools are a haven for many kids.

"Bold changes and major restructuring are needed and are finally underway at the high school. The daily student attendance rate this year now averages ninety percent, which represents an increase of almost twenty percent in the last three years. Student suspensions are at an all-time low and are now at the state average. And kids like the changes that have been put in place. They feel more welcomed at the school than ever before.

"These are not the images you associate with urban, inner-city high schools. Instead, most people envision classrooms filled with bored and disruptive students who are being taught by low-quality teachers. Although our cynics have not disappeared and there are a handful of mediocre teachers that should be replaced, there is an excitement at the school and a growing feeling among all parties that things are finally moving in the right direction."

Still pressing, John threw one more zinger at me. "Okay, that sounds fine. But suppose you are a Latino single mother and you share a rented apartment on the top floor of a 'three-decker' in Central Falls with two other families. You work two jobs and are just keeping your head above water. You enroll your ninth-grade son in Central Falls High School.

"You later learn that last year, only about half of those students entering as freshmen graduated four years later. The number of graduates that go on to college is also miniscule. To make matters worse, you read in the paper that the high school has been classified as a low-performing school for several years in a row. How happy would you be in sending your son to such a school?

"But wait, there is more. You are financially strapped and can't send your son to a private school, since neighboring public high schools aren't accepting transfer students under the parent choice option."

John had my back to the wall with his hypothetical scenario. I had to be honest.

"I would be worried. In fact, I would be quite concerned. Yes, I would be seeing red flags, with no place to turn.

"But my feeling would depend upon my son and how prepared he is to succeed in school. If he is a conscientious young man and likes school and has done well in the first eight grades, I may not be overly concerned. If he has learning problems, I would be anxious to know what type of support would be available for him.

"In the long term, even working two jobs, I would have to stay close to him and his school progress and be alert to the type of friends he makes and frequently monitor his school performance. He would definitely be on a short leash.

"If my impressions of the principal, teachers, and kids were favorable, showing me that the place is safe, well managed, and full of caring people—something I would hopefully glean on my school visits and discussion with my son's teachers—his school experience may not be as bad as you think.

"Finally, I would also want to know what major changes are being contemplated for the school and how those changes would impact my son. Of course, entering the ninth grade in any high school, not just a new school, is challenge enough for any teenager and parent, so I would pray a lot."

After I finished John laughed and said, "You really twisted that one. God, that was a long-winded evasion of the truth, dear professor."

"You're wrong. That wasn't twisting!" I argued. "The high school has some great things going for it. The large majority of kids are super kids who have a great deal of pride in their school. We have some wonderful and talented teachers who are very dedicated to their students.

Yes, we could stand more teachers like that, but as I just said, we also have those that are 'stuck in the mud,' slowing needed progress.

"Another thing. We definitely have to change the way we teach urban kids. The traditional approach, with an overdependence on teacher-directed instruction, is not working in our new world of standards-based learning. But there are hopeful signs, and the high school, I expect, will look very different and be serving students better when my son graduates four years from now."

"Hopeful signs? They have been saying that for twenty years," John replied.

"All right, John. That's enough. The only way I can convince you that real hope is on the horizon is to tell you about four students I met who graduated Central Falls High School this past year. Somehow these young people survived the obstacles low-income Latino families face and actually did extremely well in school.

"These stories give us hope for the next generation of Latino children—a hope that has to be realized by a greater number of Latino children and families. Given the projected increase of Latinos in the next few years, the future of our state and the country hangs in the balance. We have no choice; we must better educate these students, and we're running out of time."

With a wide grin on his face, John said, "Okay, professor. Nicely said, although you sound like you're giving me a lecture. But hey, I'm glad there's some positive stuff. All I hear about Central Falls is bad stuff. I'm sure there are some great kids, teachers, and parents there who really do care."

CHAPTER 2

The Obstacles to Success
in an Inner-City School

Although it is necessary to take a close look at the crusade to reform Central Falls High School and provide extensive detail on the uniqueness of the city of Central Falls and the people who live there, it is also important to learn how some recent graduates coped with life in a low-performing high school. What were their feelings, their disappointments, and their joys? Did they feel Central Falls High School had failed them?

In seeking answers to these questions, four Central Falls Latino seniors, Class of 2009, were selected and asked how they managed to succeed in a low-performing city high school.

Their stories appear in the closing chapters of this book, and as their individual stories unfold, several questions emerge.

For example, why does a small minority of students survive and even prosper in urban public schools, while a majority of others do poorly, drop out early, fail to get a high school diploma after four or more years, or somehow never seem to fully understand the future value of education and training beyond high school?

What are those factors that separate these two groups—the survivors who go on to further education and successful careers, and others who experience school failure, drop out of school, and become trapped in unskilled, low-income jobs for the rest of their lives, or even worse, become chronically unemployed? The sad part is that many of those who are trapped have untapped skills and talents that unfortunately are wasted as opportunity passes them by.

Whose fault is this? Is it the lack of high-quality urban teachers, generally poor teaching, and incompetent school leaders? Is it the protection of the status quo and the resistance to change by teachers? Is it a lack of resources and adequate facilities often observed in bleak, large, impersonal, out-of-date urban high schools, which critics have labeled "dropout factories"?

Does a good share of the blame rest with disengaged parents who, for a variety of reasons, have not been directly involved in their children's academic development? Are the depressing statistics that are linked to poverty in the inner city—statistics such as the high percentage of urban youth living below the poverty line—the major contributing factor to school failure?

Are there political, economic, or cultural and historical factors unique to Latinos at play here? Maybe all these things have a role, with different mixes depending upon the unique makeup of a particular school district.

A major purpose of the book is to shed some light on these questions as the four students and their parents tell their compelling personal stories. Through these stories, much can be learned about what it takes to raise student expectations and have students become motivated to work hard and succeed in urban schools.

In spite of unique and competing forces and conditions that discourage the majority of students in Central Falls High School from succeeding academically and realizing their dreams, a few have excelled. How did that happen?

CHAPTER 3

A Jaded Perception of Urban Schools

John's comment about suburban administrators lacking experience and knowledge about urban education needs qualification.

Many nonurban school superintendents are not totally ignorant of the Spanish culture or the issues facing low-income minority families and children. It is apparent that a growing number of suburban communities have an increasing number of low-income minority students. Teachers and administrators in these school districts must contend with the educational challenges these students present, and are now being held accountable for their academic achievement, or lack thereof, under the No Child Left Behind (NCLB) regulations.

Nonurban superintendents and principals have had other limited contacts with inner-city high schools. Many have participated in school accreditation reviews of urban high schools; however, such experiences admittedly provided them with only quick glimpses of real life within an urban school and the role cultural differences play in educating non-English-speaking children.

These experiences were in-and-out, three-day school visits, much different from working daily in an urban school and understanding the complex conditions faced by disadvantaged minority students at home, in the neighborhood, in the classroom, and on the streets.

John was right. Suburban educators are not totally familiar with the day-to-day survival of urban children and the problems poor urban children bring to school each day. Unlike students in suburban and private schools, many of whom achieve in spite of teachers, urban students may require more from their teachers. Suburban educators lack direct and extensive experience with large populations of urban students and families and may not fully understand the intricacies of teaching in an urban school.

But suburban educators do know one thing—teaching in urban schools requires a special kind of dedication and commitment. They know this because most of them have a small percentage of low-income minority students in their classrooms who present the same type of learning problems as inner-city students do.

It may only be ten percent and not fifty percent of the student body, but nonetheless, these are low-achieving students who eventually drop out of school, have minimal parental support, or have personal issues that interfere with their learning. As with their urban counterparts, finding solutions is not easy. Suburban educators fully realize how difficult it is to teach these low-achieving students.

The general public, however, has a jaded perception of urban schools, particularly the secondary schools. They are seen as tough places, depressing and threatening and located in crime-infested neighborhoods. The school buildings are dark, dingy, and uninviting. They look like old relics: too large, poorly equipped, poorly maintained, and lacking in resources.

By the time students reach high school, they have such low skill levels and a history of failure that hopelessness has already set in. It is just a matter of time before they become dropouts or "pushouts."

The general impression is that too many urban teachers are marking time and are not interested in changing their old teaching habits. High school teachers appear frustrated with students who come to them with defeatist attitudes and reading and math levels three to four years below grade level. Many of these students sit passively in their classes, waiting for time to pass before they can legally drop out of school. These teachers have incredibly difficult jobs.

Urban administrators are perceived for the most part as being managers and not instructional leaders. Few play both roles well. Some have no clue about how to improve instruction. They are bogged down with demands from the central office and state bureaucracies and a myriad of school management and discipline issues, some of which are unique to minority inner-city students.

Many of our urban schools (and suburban ones too) are clearly organized for the adults who work there and not for children. It would, however, be less than honest not to mention that in spite of recent major strides in reforming public education, these problems haven't totally disappeared and are still evident today in a large number of inner-city high schools.

The image of urban high schools as dropout factories has been front-page news in recent years. It is a perception the general public now has, and one that is also held by nonurban educators who have never taught in an urban school.

An example of how such perceptions develop is illustrated by the story of a suburban superintendent of schools who chaired an accreditation visit to South Boston High School during the desegregation days in the 1970s, the controversial period when forced busing was used as a method to racially balance schools. At the time, Judge W. Arthur Garrity had fired the principal and taken unprecedented judicial control of the school.

The superintendent remembers visiting South Boston Headmaster Jerry Wynegar one rainy day in late March for a preliminary visit. It was a while after a black student had stabbed a white student, but racial tension was still present in the building, even though white and black students no longer had to enter the school through different doors.

The number of uniformed police in the building had been reduced from a high of approximately one hundred at the peak of the racial crisis to twenty-five or so security guards.

When entering his office, Jerry greeted the superintendent coldly. It was obvious that Jerry felt it was ludicrous for "Southie" to undergo a formal school evaluation; in his opinion, it was a waste of time. He reported directly to Judge Garrity and no one else; however, pressure from downtown won out and he was forced to host an evaluation committee.

It didn't help that there was only one minority member on the visiting committee, and she was a middle-class black language teacher from the affluent Boston suburb of Newton. Fortunately, after the committee had spent three days in his school, Jerry cooled down, accepted the inevitable, and things went well.

Three things happened during the three days in South Boston High School that have had a profound effect to this very day on the superintendent's feelings about racial discrimination and the lack of educational opportunity for poor minority students who attend urban high schools.

After he finished his initial planning meeting with Jerry and returned to his car, he got caught in a torrential downpour and discovered that his battery was dead. Soaking wet, he ran back into the school and discovered that everyone had left except for a black guidance counselor who greeted him in the school lobby.

He asked him if he had jumper cables and could he help him start his car. The counselor asked him where his car was parked; the superintendent told him he was parked on a side street off G Street.

The superintendent will never forget the counselor's response to his request, when he said, "I'm terribly sorry, but as much as I would like to help you out, I can't. If I'm spotted on that street helping a white man start his car, I'm taking a huge risk and could suffer bodily harm. It's a rough neighborhood, and a number of nasty, violent things have happened there recently. You've got to understand that this school is an oasis for black folks like me. I feel safe here, but not out there. My car is parked on the side of the school building in the fenced area for faculty parking, where it is easily accessible and allows me to quickly get out of South Boston after school. Believe me, I don't hang around too long."

The next day the visiting superintendent was at the high school early and witnessed a sight that has also been indelibly etched in his mind. He heard the loud roar of ten motorcycles driven by rugged-looking, armed white policemen with their lily-white helmets, jet-black uniforms, and shiny brown leather boots. They were escorting ten buses of black students from Roxbury to South Boston High School.

It was surreal. As he watched the black students walk en masse through the front door, he looked intently at their serious-looking faces and saw no smiles and heard no laughter. It was obvious they didn't want to come to Southie.

The last memory the superintendent had is a visual image of an old, dismal, large city high school building with antiquated facilities and equipment that were supposed to adequately support modern educational programs and practices for urban students.

Although rich in tradition and fondly remembered by the Irish who went there, South Boston High School was such a building, a true relic having outlived its usefulness long before the school accreditation visit.

On the last day of the visitation, the superintendent found himself talking to several black students outside the gym locker room. They were talking about an exceptionally tall, black ninth-grade basketball phenom from Cambridge Rindge and Latin named Patrick Ewing, whom they predicted would be the next Wilt Chamberlain. The superintendent noticed that their jerseys were soaked in sweat and asked them why they didn't take showers after gym class.

One skinny student who resembled a young Eddie Murphy spoke up. "Hey man, haven't you seen the locker room? Take a look inside and you'll get your answers about this place." He entered the locker room accompanied by "Eddie" and another black student with the odd nickname of "Pay Dirt."

What the superintendent saw spoke volumes about the inequities in public education. It was a dingy, dirty, tiny room totally inadequate to accommodate the slightly over six hundred male students in the school. There were only two shower stalls, and both showers had been inoperable for months as a maintenance request gathered dust downtown in some central office file.

What shocked him was that "Eddie" and his friends accepted this sorry situation, and he wondered if this was symbolic of other phases of their school experience. If so, urban minority students were being shortchanged in every aspect of their educational experience while more affluent suburban school students like those in his school district enjoyed so many more advantages.

It is not surprising that the court ruling to desegregate Boston schools from 1975 through 1988 was a major cause of "white flight" to surrounding suburbs, resulting in Boston's public schools today serving mainly black, Hispanic, and other minority children while white enrollment has dropped to just fourteen percent.

What has been created are two public school systems separated by race, class, and wealth. One is for the low-income urban youngsters, and the other for the more privileged middle-class white students. No wonder there is a student achievement gap and unequal educational opportunity.

CHAPTER 4

An Urban Principal Questions Dropout Figures

The stereotypical image of urban high schools is not always accurate. Central Falls High School is not a threatening place where violence could strike at any moment. In fact, it is a warm, friendly place with courteous and well-behaved students, about two-thirds of them from Latino families.

The main building is old and resources like computer technology are limited, but there is clear evidence that most teachers care deeply about their students, and administrators are doing their best to promote school improvement.

However, the results are not there. Poor attendance, chronic tardiness, dismal state assessment scores, low graduation rates, and high dropout rates have plagued the school for years. As time goes on, questions are being raised about what caused this gridlock, this cycle of failure, this inability to raise the achievement level of students.

Poverty and cultural differences play a key role; however, the general public and many critics of urban education do not always understand the complexities or the specifics, if you will, of why Latino students are not achieving at the level and rate they should.

It took an article in the *Providence Journal* written by columnist Mark Patinkin to best describe the barriers that Latino students and urban educators must overcome if sustainable progress is to be made in raising student achievement. Mark interviewed Fred Silva, the principal of Tolman High School in neighboring Pawtucket, an inner-city school with a student body that is fifty percent Hispanic and where sixty percent of the students qualified for free or reduced-price lunch.

Patinkin mentioned that he had seldom seen a principal speak so clearly about the real story behind the dropout rates.

In the article, Silva expressed concern that the high number of dropouts at his school didn't reflect how great his kids were and how much they had to deal with on an everyday basis. He claimed that the dropout figures were inflated and explained why.

He spoke about how today's immigrants are much different from the Irish, Italian, and other immigrants of years ago. If you came from Italy, you had to work hard to learn the language and become Americanized. You had no choice, since you had lost contact with your old homeland.

Today, Silva said, immigrants come for a better life, too, but their connections to their old county are stronger. He said, "Planes make it easy to go back and forth, e-mail and cell phones keep families in contact outside the borders, and the Internet brings them news from home."

Silva mentioned how television used to teach English to newcomers. Now, he says, "You can be living in Pawtucket while watching local channels from Portugal, Turkey, or the Caribbean. That means that it is harder to teach English, because kids are not immersed in it at home. Often that means students aren't able to keep up with school, or aren't ready to graduate, and that adds to the dropout rate."

It gets even more complex. Silva then mentioned a problem that few outside of education are aware of, a problem that Central Falls High School faces every year. He said it is common for students from the Caribbean countries to go home for Christmas and stay for several months. By the time the kids return, they've been listed as dropouts.

The problem Silva alludes to needs further explanation. While designing a more stringent high school attendance policy in Central Falls, the problem of students missing a month or more of schooling was a major issue and required the school to conduct a series of public meetings and directly communicate with all parents in an attempt to inform them of the dangers of disrupting their children's education for that length of time.

On the surface, you would think the problem would be simple to solve. However, you need to understand the importance of the family unit to Latinos. According to research done by the Rhode Island Office of Minority Health, Latino families are seen as being broadly defined, close knit, and emotionally and financially supportive. Their ties to their relatives in their native countries and its culture are particularly strong.

The close family unit referred to as "familismo" often includes non-blood-related persons. Latinos tend to view the family as a primary source of support and share strong bonds of loyalty. The dignity of each individual, a hierarchical order among siblings, and a duty to care for family members are valued. According to one study, Latino adolescents are more inclined than white students to adopt their parents' commitment to religious and political beliefs, occupational preferences, and lifestyles.

The characteristic of "personalismo" is also evident. This refers to the tendency of Latinos to place utmost value on individuals as opposed to institutions. They tend to trust and cooperate with individuals they know personally and with whom they have warm, friendly, and affectionate relationships. Personal space is close and frequently shared with family members or close friends. Politeness and respect are highly valued, and children are taught to respect their elders and the authority figures within the community.

The male is usually perceived as dominant and strong, whereas the female is perceived as nurturing and self-sacrificing. Latinos may get agitated or emotional at times and become quite animated in conversations—a behavior frequently misperceived as being "out of control." Their voice pitch and inflections are often misinterpreted as confrontational even though most Latinos in fact avoid confrontation and criticism.

Many immigrant Latino parents received a limited education in their native countries, and the little they received was of poor quality. Many are illiterate in their native language.

For example, a study by the Inter-American Development Bank revealed that only one in three Latin Americans (or about thirty-three percent) manages to obtain a secondary school education, while in Southeast Asia the number is eighty percent.

Another study indicated that students in Colombia, El Salvador, and Peru who work and go to school labor some twenty hours a week while in school, and thirty-two hours a week when on vacation. In rural zones, there is a marked drop in school attendance during harvest time, and often peasant children even leave school for five or six years and

then return for a short time before dropping out and permanently joining the agricultural labor force.

Researchers contend that the heart of the education problem in Latin
America is its prevailing low quality. At an international conference on
education reform in Latin America held in Toronto a few years ago, it
was emphasized that the real problem was not access to education, but
rather its poor quality.

Although graduation rates have risen in Latin American countries,
instruction in basic subjects like language, mathematics, and the sciences has eroded. The biggest problem stems from the teaching in the
public schools, where in general teachers are not well paid and fewer
instructional hours are required as compared to private schools that
serve middle- and upper-class students.

The educational level of a child's parents is unquestionably one of
the major predictors of a child's future success in school. The high
number of illiterate parents and those with only a few years of primary
education currently residing in Central Falls and Pawtucket presents a
major challenge to urban educators in those communities.

Fred Silva understands the nuances of urban school problems. He
faces those problems every day. He is in one of the most difficult positions in education. At the same time, if you asked him, he would tell
you that it is one of the most personally fulfilling and important jobs
anyone can have.

CHAPTER 5

Residential Instability among Latinos

The bulk of the immigrants who move to Central Falls and Pawtucket to join their friends and relatives are unskilled laborers with a limited education. English is not the primary language spoken in the home. Economic survival, not education, is their priority.

Although many place a high value on a quality education for their children, too many do not, because putting bread on the table and finding affordable and suitable housing sap most of their time, money, energy, and worry.

A 2008 report by the US Conference of Mayors stated that poverty, unemployment, and the lack of affordable housing were the primary causes of homelessness and hunger for families in surveyed cities.

To quote the report, "At a time when the United States faces one of the biggest economic downturns in its history, the issues of hunger and homelessness are more prevalent than ever." Cities reported an eye-popping twelve percent increase in these areas in 2008 alone. The tenants of rental units in buildings where the landlord faced foreclosure were the most vulnerable to becoming homeless, the report said.

BAD TIMES IN CENTRAL FALLS

It is 2010 and things have only gotten worse, especially in the tiny city of Central Falls. Foreclosures are spiking and unemployment is fifteen percent, with a high of slightly over sixteen percent in June 2009. Fran Gallo, the school superintendent, reports that due to the foreclosures, student enrollment has dropped by four hundred students after several years of stable enrollment.

She recommends walking the narrow city streets and looking up at the domineering sight of the tired-looking three- and four-story tenement buildings that densely line both sides of the streets.

Gallo was right. Walking around one small block, you see several lifeless apartment buildings with plywood nailed over the windows and doors.

When you ride around the city, you observe many other empty buildings that are boarded up and you wonder where the families went. Have they moved in with relatives elsewhere? Are three or four families living together in two-bedroom apartments? Have they returned to their native countries? You might wonder what the effect an economy gone sour has on an unemployed Latino mother who is trying to raise her children alone in this city.

FAMILIES IN FLIGHT

The combination of poverty, high unemployment, and lack of affordable housing causes "families in flight." Such is the case in Central Falls.

Fred Silva put it best when he said, "Until I came to Tolman High, I never realized how often some families move. People in unskilled jobs face frequent layoffs, and if they find a new job across state, they'll move to be near it."

Fred explained that if his school is able to show that students who have left are enrolled in a new high school, they're considered transfer students. But as any urban school administrator will tell you, some families are hard to track, so their children end up listed as dropouts.

It is common for new students in Central Falls to have already been through three or more transfers. Silva indicated that he had one student who counted Tolman as her fourteenth school. Sometimes these are foster or group home kids whose lives are in constant flux.

Often, unskilled Latino immigrants who arrive in the United States are surprised to learn that they have not escaped poverty and that realizing the American Dream is not as possible as it was for European immigrants years ago. Still they persist and send as much money as they can back to struggling relatives in their homeland.

Roberto Suro, in his book *Strangers Among Us*, explains why Latino immigrants face the hard reality that upward social mobility is not like it used to be in earlier generations. He writes, "Whereas Irish and Italians were able to climb a generational stepladder from canal diggers to factory workers to white-collar professionals, in Information Age America the middle rungs are missing. Because Latinos are poorly educated, they have a particularly difficult challenge in getting a foothold on the ladder in the New Economy."

Suro argues that there is not the same "level playing field" that existed for immigrants years ago. He feels Latinos are locked in poverty because of the American economy, a changing society, and a lack of good public education and social services, a claim that has been repeated by a number of sociologists. He further contends that unions, churches, and schools have failed Latinos.

Suro's critics have difficulty in fully accepting all his assumptions; however, his thesis about the New Economy and the low educational level of Latino immigrants as barriers to upward social mobility can't be denied.

The forecasts by the Bureau of Labor Statistics about job growth in the next ten years further illustrate how difficult it will be for poorly educated, low-skilled Latinos to find a foothold in the New Economy.

Although jobs are projected to be plentiful in such key areas as finance, engineering, health-related fields, computer science, information science, and management-information systems, simply having a degree in one of these subjects may not be enough, according to Diana Middleton, a reporter for the *Wall Street Journal*. "Not all of the jobs in those areas will be 'techie' in nature," she says. "Companies will be looking for employers with multiple skill sets."

In her 2009 article entitled "Landing a Job in the Future Takes a Two-Track Mind," Middleton provides numerous illustrations where this rising phenomenon is evident, such as in green technology, where engineers who can mastermind high-voltage electric grids are needed, and in nursing, where licensed nurses who have additional certificates or advanced degrees in risk management and/or in nursing informatics will be in greater demand.

This increased demand for degrees in these growing fields, coupled with the need for further skills in emerging new areas, is requiring a highly educated and multiskilled workforce. Such change places a greater premium on new knowledge and gaining the necessary education in order to seize the opportunity to pursue a successful career.

Unfortunately, unless the educational achievement of Latinos in this country increases dramatically in the next few years, the missing "middle rungs" on the socioeconomic ladder will increase in number, making it even more difficult for Latinos to climb out of poverty, locate well-paying jobs, and realize their dreams for a better life.

It also means that many unemployed Latinos will remain in constant motion, moving from one locale to another looking for employment opportunities and suitable housing for their families.

Rather than straddle two worlds, many Latinos return to their native countries, especially if they have close relatives still living there. Other immigrants have no intention of becoming American citizens, but migrate to the United States for short periods of time to bank money for their families and then return to their native country.

Wages in their own country are so low that the opportunity to work in a low-skilled job for the hourly rate paid by American businesses becomes an attractive alternative. The Pew Hispanic Center estimates that approximately twenty-five percent of Hispanic immigrants, many undocumented, have no intention of remaining here permanently.

Fred Silva provides a telling illustration of another phenomenon that he feels also inflates his school's dropout statistics. "I have seen students who arrive in the middle of the school year from places like the Dominican Republic. Part of their goal is to learn enough English to be able to work in the tourist industry back home. When they feel they're ready, they head back, and again, those kids are considered dropouts."

Regardless of the reason, the effect that family residential instability has on student academic achievement is not thoroughly understood by the officials who publish dropout statistics or by those in the media who sensationalize accounts about how poorly the urban high school "dropout factories" are serving low-income minority students.

Unless you work in urban schools like teachers and administrators do, you cannot thoroughly comprehend how difficult it is to raise student achievement when students are constantly transferring in from other schools or from other countries, while others are leaving because of a change of residence or simply dropping out. This problem is further compounded if student attendance is sporadic and tardiness rates are high.

For example, with the opening of school in September 2006, there were over three hundred student changes (new transfers plus leavers) in Central Falls High School in a total population at that time of 950 students. There were nearly one thousand student changes among a total district enrollment of 3800 students.

Unquestionably, when students move frequently from school to school, many during the same school year, their chances of doing well in school are severely diminished.

Research has also demonstrated that immigrant children who arrive in the United States before the age of ten do better academically than those who arrive after that age, especially if those who arrive earlier remain in a stable environment for most of their early education.

Gene Maeroff, in his 2006 book *Building Blocks,* points to empirical evidence that speaks to the critical importance of the pre-K through third grade as a proving ground for the ability of schools to absorb immigrant children and provide them with a worthy education. Those early school years are the time to integrate and align learning and have children develop the habits and dispositions that will last a lifetime.

Maeroff contends that students who complete the third grade as poor readers face an almost certain struggle for the remainder of their education. He also says that it is the time to build a foundation for mathematics, or "students will flounder in high school, avoid math in college, and cut themselves off from careers in fields demanding knowledge of math."

While talking with school administrators in Chelsea, Massachusetts, a few years ago, it was learned that they track student achievement in two ways. One method measures student progress for all students yearly, while the other method measures only those students who remained in the district for their twelve years of schooling.

Not surprisingly, the students who remained for the full twelve years did significantly better in school than those who transferred in at other points on the pre-K–12 grade continuum.

The Chelsea example is most telling. The foundation, or building blocks, Latino students establish in those early years must be solid.

Unfortunately, over time many of those students move to other school districts, while new transfers from other districts move in, their previous preparation for learning generally unknown. To further complicate matters, a high percentage of those students may also be special education and English-language learners.

As mentioned previously, the high number of such yearly changes in inner-city districts far exceeds those of suburban districts. Because of such urban mobility, the accountability for ninth graders who drop out of Central Falls High School has to be shared with multiple school districts.

Undoubtedly, tracking the achievement of students who complete all twelve years in their school system makes sense and provides valuable feedback. On the other hand, it also provides an assessment of a district's adaptability and capacity to design successful programs to accommodate a high percentage of transfer students and put them on the right track to school success. This, of course, takes additional resources in a time when states and local communities are faced with shrinking revenue.

Obviously, there are many variables other than residential instability that skew student achievement results; however, the point is clear. The disruption and discontinuity caused by frequent school changes in a child's early education greatly reduces the chances of his or her school success and eventual attainment of high school and college diplomas.

It can then be concluded that the earlier a non-English-speaking immigrant child enters school in the United States and the longer that child remains in the same school system for his or her elementary and secondary education, the greater his or her chances are for school success.

Why the media and state and federal education officials have not given more weight to residential instability as a major cause for the high number of inner-city school dropouts is puzzling. Instead, they are stuck on labeling low-performing schools as "failing schools needing correction" and "dropout factories" pushing kids out the door without their diplomas.

When the headlines read that one in ten high schools fall into the "dropout factories" category, it is also mentioned that "most of them are in the inner city with high proportions of minority students." Unfortunately, such statements stigmatize all urban high schools where students of color are enrolled, including those that are functioning well or are earnestly undergoing significant reform.

That type of stereotyping is counterproductive and accomplishes little. In fact, it is a disservice to those committed professionals in urban public schools who have spent their lives teaching low-income minority children.

Fred Silva is right when he contends that the "dropout factory" label obscures what his teachers are up against and how important their work is in a school like his. It is his final words at the end of the newspaper article that really resonate. He says that the biggest disservice of all is that "the dropout figures don't reflect how great our kids are and how much they have overcome." He is so right.

CHAPTER 6

The Role of Poverty

The social scientists tell us that poverty is an exceptionally complicated phenomenon. One simplistic explanation, however, still exists—the poor cause their own poverty.

How often do you hear someone say, "I grew up poor and we made it. We didn't even know we were poor." Or better still, "My grandfather arrived in this country at the age of sixteen from Italy. He couldn't speak a word of English, but that didn't stop him from becoming a successful and wealthy businessman and sending his three children to fine colleges."

Isn't that what America is all about? Isn't it the land of opportunity, where the Statue of Liberty's welcoming inscription reads in part, "Give me your tired, your poor, your huddled masses. . ."? Anything is possible in America if you work hard enough.

The "blame the poor" perception is not applicable to all members of the lower class. Most poor people are able and willing to work hard if given the chance, and would prefer to work rather than receive welfare payments. Unfortunately, the low wages paid to unskilled workers and the lack of access to education makes it difficult for them to move to higher-paying jobs.

We now see an increasing number of single women in poverty who are heads of households. There are more unwanted births, divorces, and separations, and accompanying all these is an increase in the number of fathers who are skipping child support payments.

In 2008, Central Falls led the state in births to teenaged mothers (ages fifteen to seventeen) with an average of sixty per one thousand children. In 2006, Central Falls led the state with forty-one percent of children under eighteen living below the poverty line; the state average was seventeen percent.

Poverty places incredible stress on young people and their families, and that leads to other problems. The Rhode Island Institute for the Study and Practice of Nonviolence reports that there is an increased rate of violence in places where there are concentrations of poor and unemployed people, crowded housing, residential instability, and family disruption. Through the use of conflict mediation and other strategies, the institute has been successful in hiring streetworkers (one works with Central Falls High School) who provide coordinated support and services to victims of violent crimes in order to stem later retaliation by the victims.

In spite of efforts to reduce violence, Kids Count, a respected Rhode Island affiliate of a nationally recognized data bank, reported that from 2006 to 2008, just over twenty percent of children in Central Falls had an incarcerated parent as compared to a state average of eleven percent, while the number of abused children in Central Falls in 2008 was approximately seventeen percent higher than the state average.

Latinos who grow up in poverty also suffer a greater incidence of health problems. Children raised in poverty tend to miss school more because of illness. According to several health organizations, these children have a much higher rate of accidents than do other children, and they are twice as likely to have impaired vision and hearing, iron deficiency anemia, and higher-than-normal levels of lead in the blood, which can impair brain function.

The Rhode Island Department of Health reports that the overall state population has better maternal and child health care outcomes than the Hispanic population; for example, over twelve percent of pregnant Hispanic women have delayed prenatal care against a state average of nine percent. They also report that the rates of gonorrhea and tuberculosis cases in the Hispanic population are considerably higher than those in the overall state population.

Issues of poverty therefore directly relate to poor school performance by Latino students. Breaking out of the cycle of poverty is not easy for Latino young people and their families, who find themselves trapped in untenable living situations.

It raises important questions about future generations of Latinos. Will high-quality teachers and high-quality teaching by themselves free low-income students from the shackles of poverty and propel them to school success and more promising futures? Is education the answer, a sure pathway to the American dream? If so, we are not doing too well at this point in time.

CHAPTER 7

The Need for Better Teaching

If you listened to the critics of public education, you would be convinced that the major reason Latino kids are not graduating from high school is because the schools and the teachers are lousy. It's as simple as that. Hire better teachers and get rid of the "dead wood," and you will get positive results.

Let's assume that the best teachers in the country are hired. To what degree could they overcome disengaged and uninterested parents, the issues of poverty, and the cultural and historical barriers that block student achievement? What are realistic targets of improvement? How long would it take and how much would it cost to really raise the achievement bar? Of course, there is another cost now, a very high human cost.

There is no question that the status quo is unacceptable and the expectations for students, teachers, and parents must be raised much higher than they are now. It is apparent to those knowledgeable about urban education that instruction must be more rigorous, interactive, and relevant.

Too many low-income students are failing and not getting an education that leads anywhere. But can good teachers and good teaching do it by themselves?

One thing is certain. Teachers can do little to significantly improve the quality of life for impoverished families. They can't stop a family from relocating five times in four years with children who have missed chunks of schooling during those transitions. Yes, they can improve student literacy skills, but if the primary language at home for eighty percent of the students is something other than English, delayed literacy occurs, and it affects their school performance.

In a school district where over one quarter of your students are English-language learners and another quarter are special education students, how can you make the costly accommodations necessary for those students when budgets are tight, staffing is limited, and your regular education students require considerable attention?

Urban school officials and teachers shudder when they see how badly urban schools are underfunded by state legislatures, as inequity in funding of education continues unabated.

Creative outreach to parents can be initiated and parent engagement in their child's education increased; however, many Latino parents are busy working two jobs, have limited time, and distrust schools, having had poor, limited experiences in school themselves. However, the role parents play in making the education of their children a priority in their lives cannot be underestimated. There is a future payoff for those parents who make the personal sacrifices needed to become directly and actively involved in their child's schooling.

Charter schools excel in parent engagement, and their students reap the benefits. Their schools, however, are much smaller with fewer students, and there is a built-in selectivity factor at work too. Immigrant parents who want to send their children to a private urban charter school are representative of the small percentage of parents who are usually already actively engaged in their child's education.

School reformers suggest that urban public schools ought to follow the lead of charter schools and require parents to sign contracts committing them to accepting certain responsibilities while their child is enrolled in school.

The contract idea is a good one, as is the suggestion to have individual learning plans developed for every school-aged child. However, what do you do with the parents who violate their contract? Send them to another school district?

When teachers complain that the general public and local and state government officials don't understand the challenges of teaching low-income minority children, they are often accused of covering up their own incompetence, or "copping out." That is unfair and insulting to the majority of dedicated teachers in the inner cities of our country.

However, in spite of this criticism and the obstacles they face, a case can be made that urban teachers must teach better. To do this, they have to think differently about how they are currently teaching urban students.

A case in point is Central Falls High School. In 2002, the high school received its accreditation report from the New England Association of Schools and Colleges. The report followed a three-day visit by a team of teachers who looked at the entire school operation using a set of seven standards that ranged from the quality of curriculum and instruction to adequacy of school facilities.

The report was helpful but limited. It commended the students and how "warm, orderly, friendly, and respectful they were in their relationships with the school staff."

In the areas of curriculum and instruction, the report lacked specifics and included vague pedagogical phrases, like "There is a need to develop schoolwide academic expectations for student learning," and recommendations like "Develop and implement curricula, in all academic areas that correlate with state frameworks, national standards, and the school mission and academic expectations for student learning."

Because of concern about the overall quality of the school, full accreditation of the high school was delayed until 2007, when the school submitted its five-year follow-up report and announced its plans to restructure the school with the direct assistance of and at the insistence of the Rhode Island State Department of Education.

The major failure of the accreditation report was that it told little about exactly what type of teaching was taking place in classrooms, especially in literacy, math, and special education.

There were no specific statements regarding the quality of the teachers, their successful or unsuccessful teaching and assessment practices, or how rigorous and effective their instruction was.

Straightforward answers were needed to some basic questions, like "How proficient were Central Falls High School students in reading, writing, and math? What are we doing right and what are we doing wrong?"

As Ted Sizer, the late Harvard and Brown University educational reformer used to say, "The major purpose of schools is to make students think and think well." Was this happening at Central Falls High

School? It wasn't until the State Department of Education undertook an instructional audit in 2007 that answers to that question were forthcoming.

Unlike the accreditation review, where all aspects of the school program were reviewed, the state's instructional audit, also termed the Commissioner's Review, was more focused on curriculum, instruction, student learning, and the quality and results of teaching, especially in literacy and math.

Another difference was the makeup of the evaluation team. It included thirty-two team members consisting of State Department of Education instructional specialists and highly qualified urban teachers and administrators with successful experience in inner-city schools. Virtually every high school teacher was observed teaching, as the team logged a total of 128 hours of classroom observation.

When the final report was received, one statement stood out. Similar to the accreditation report, it mentioned the friendly and welcoming culture that permeated the school, and teachers were commended for their collegiality and dedication to their students.

But then it read, "*A culture based primarily on caring is not enough. Where such a culture dominates, neither teachers nor students are challenged to improve nor are they held to high expectations. Such is the case in Central Falls High School.*"

One needed to read further to see if such a shocking statement was supported by sufficient data gathered through direct observations and discussion with students, teachers, and administrators, and a review of student assessment data.

Were teachers so caring that they were not challenging students, accepting only a minimum, "get by" effort? Were students stuck in whole-class, teacher-directed instruction where the focus was on lecture, drill, seatwork, and low-level skills?

Were students passive or highly interactive in learning? What type, degree, and quality of interaction between teacher and students and between student and student were actually occurring? Were complex issues being raised where teachers were asking open-ended questions? These and other questions came to mind.

The ultimate criticism, although felt to be unfair by some high school teachers, was difficult to rebut because it was given by a selected group of highly respected, experienced, and knowledgeable urban teachers and subject specialists.

Their comments were from accomplished peers, not suburban teachers selected at random. The criticism was hard-hitting but constructive, and directed at both students and teachers without the type of ambiguous language often used by educators. The following is a sample:

- Although students' literacy skills vary significantly, the majority of students do not read or write well. Many students are hampered by their lack of basic literacy skills, interest, and confidence, and often say that what they learn to read and write will not be helpful or relevant beyond the school walls.
- A few students do produce high-quality writing. When they share it with their peers and teachers, they receive respectful feedback, but it does not tend to push them to think critically about writing. Very few students know how to use rubrics to critically improve their writing or to give critical feedback to their peers.
- While there are a few students who understand and apply mathematics well, most students are not proficient in math. Many lack basic mathematical skills or the knowledge to apply those skills. They even struggle with basic math warm-ups, rely heavily on calculators for even simple tasks, and do not move into more complex math.
- Students perceive math as an isolated topic and are not clear about the value of learning it. Most students say they need to know math to get a job, but it is unclear whether the math they refer to means anything other than basic arithmetic computations.
- With this limited view, they do not look for or see essential mathematical concepts, big mathematical ideas, or the relevance of these concepts and ideas in other disciplines. They therefore lack an essential set of tools to analyze and solve a wide variety of real-world problems.

The next criticisms were directed at teachers and confirmed the opinion that urban teachers, as dedicated as they are, must structure their classrooms differently and change some of their long-held, traditional teaching practices.

The report called for teachers to design their lessons and teach in ways that assure that their students are interested and engaged in learning, rather than having them sit passively in classrooms, being compliant and orderly, unprepared for class, and complaining that what they are learning is not preparing them well for their lives after high school.

The evaluators did see some teachers engaging their students, redesigning their lessons in order to differentiate learning and teaching in their classrooms, and giving students the opportunity to be active learners. However, in spite of their existence, it was not the norm across the school, as the following criticisms suggest:

- Many teachers over-rely on teacher-directed instruction that fails to connect to student needs and interests. Teachers often micromanage student learning by giving them detailed notes to copy from the board, stressing answers over questions, asking questions only at the literal level, stressing summary and recall, and simplifying lessons. Their expectations for responses are generally short, simple sentences rather than analytical, interpretive responses that require students to reflect upon and apply what they know. They often inhibit inquiry by telling students the correct outcome before they start to problem solve. Too often, teachers say that students are not capable and cannot be expected to do challenging work.
- Although there are a few notable exceptions, most teachers do not instruct or communicate in a way that allows their students to read and write proficiently or understand the importance of, or feel an enthusiasm for either writing or reading. To the contrary, they give superficial assignments in reading and writing that do not deepen student understanding of the topic or material and give assignments that require short, perfunctory responses, which results in mechanical completion of work rather than proficiency. . . . more importantly, they do not hold students accountable for producing quality work, for improving their work, or even for completing their work.
- Math instruction does not move students toward proficiency. Most teachers do not use questioning as a powerful tool for promoting critical thinking and understanding. Instead, they empha-

size answers and correctness. Most lessons are not designed or implemented in ways that lead from a set of initial ideas to more complex understandings, nor are they designed to build missing knowledge or skills in students. They rarely create situations where students can learn math at appropriate levels of rigor, and over-rely on whole-class instruction; therefore, some students get lost and others get bored.

Teachers understandably took issue with some of the criticism, citing some of the challenges they face when poorly prepared ninth graders land on their doorstep. They mentioned receiving students with serious deficits in basic literacy and math skills, and the time and resources it takes to bring these students up to grade level.

They pointed to the turnover in students that occurs every year, the poor student attendance, the lack of parent engagement, and the unstable leadership and lack of direction in the school.

They spoke of the desperate need for a special, individualized program for ninth graders to "ramp up" their basic academic skills through new remediation programs and strategies. The program was eventually to be housed in a separate school and provide intense academic support and personal encouragement to ninth graders, helping ease their transition into the last three years of high school.

The teacher suggestions had merit and would eventually be adopted; however, the need for many of the teachers to change and improve their teaching couldn't be denied. This too became a priority in reform efforts at the high school.

CHAPTER 8

The Blame Game

The question "Is It Poverty or Better Teaching?" has been posed by many urban school reformers. Clearly, poverty and the quality of teaching are both major reasons inner-city schools are low performing and contribute to a persistent problem that has now expanded into a national crisis. However, there are differing opinions on how much each factor is at fault.

For example, although it is apparent that urban teachers could do a better job of adapting their instruction to diverse learners, connecting it more to higher education and the workplace, and setting higher student expectations for Latino students, it is not the fault of urban teachers and school administrators that so many ninth graders drop out of school, according to Robert Balfanz and Nettie Legters, who head the Talent Development High Schools program at Johns Hopkins University.

Balfanz and Legters feel that teachers and administrators "care a lot, but they are often overmatched by the immense challenges they face." They mention that eighty percent of ninth graders in the nation's "dropout factories" can be overage for grade, repeating the grade, in need of special education services, or have math and reading skills below a seventh grade level.

They explain, "Students have the ability, but they need much more intensive and effective instruction and adult support than the high-poverty, comprehensive high school, with current levels of resources, typically provides."

In a 2009 survey taken by the Pew Hispanic Center, when Latino students were asked why they do not do as well as other students in school, they didn't blame teachers or administrators either. Instead, they blamed poor parenting and poor English skills. Ninety percent of a sample of over two thousand respondents said that a college education is important to success in life, yet only half that number said they planned to get a college degree.

According to the research data, their low expectations were due to financial pressures to support their families, poor English skills, and feeling they didn't need further education for the careers they wanted.

In the final analysis, playing the blame game is an unproductive exercise. There are multiple factors that contribute to the educational gap between whites and Latinos and the high dropout rate of Latinos—one in five Latino teens drops out of high school, twice the rate for black students and more than three times the rate of white students.

You must ask yourself what causes these problems. Is it low expectations, lack of confidence, poor English, cultural differences, segregation of inner-city minority students, or teachers who care, but settle for less from their needy students?

What about the attitudes and efforts of the students themselves? Don't they have to share some of the blame? One student interviewed recently said, "Don't blame the teachers, a lot of the kids don't even try." Where do such attitudes come from?

Is it high transiency and housing displacement, increased crime, lack of parental interest and involvement in their child's schooling, unemployment, health issues, and high rate of birth to teenage girls? Isn't it all of these things?

When you list all the possible causes, it is difficult to place specific blame on any one thing, since many of the contributing factors are interrelated.

However, we do know that there is empirical evidence that shows a near perfect linear relationship between a high school's poverty level and its tendency to lose large numbers of low-income minority students between ninth and twelfth grades, especially when they attend segregated inner-city high schools.

High poverty is definitely a major inhibitor that impedes progress in closing the achievement gap between Latinos and whites. As poverty increases in our inner cities, as economic problems remain unsolved, and as our school resources shrink, it will be even more difficult to turn low-performing high schools around.

Notice the word "difficult" is used and not the word "impossible." In spite of the odds, there are urban educators still "laboring in the vineyards" who feel that improved teaching and redesign of inner-city high schools can go a long way in reducing the dropout rate and increasing high school graduation rates. These committed teachers and administrators believe that all children can learn and that poverty is not a barrier to student achievement that can't be overcome.

These are the teachers who do not settle for students who don't work hard and only contribute the minimum. Their academic expectations for their students are high, and they push students to achieve and not take the easy road. They don't "dumb down" their teaching.

"All students will graduate" is the norm in their school. Parents are required to become actively involved in the child's school, even if they have to sign personal contracts. These teachers know it is a hard road to travel with many pitfalls, but they never give up and are never satisfied with the status quo. After years of teaching, they are still learning and are open to new ways that will bring their students academic success.

Nationwide, there has been a growing number of encouraging stories, particularly in small urban schools, typically with three hundred or more students, that provide students with an energized faculty and a higher degree of personalization and instruction, which in turn leads to substantially higher student achievement and graduation rates.

Central Falls High School has set its sights on being one of these success stories and has aggressively sought the resources and expertise to accomplish the task. However, how long will it take? Past attempts at reform have come up short, although there have recently been small signs of progress. What has to happen in Central Falls to really turn this chronically failing high school around?

CHAPTER 9

The Unique City of Central Falls

If you look at the city's website, it contains a heading that says, "A City with a Bright Future." Unfortunately, a recent feature story written by Karen Ziner in the Sunday edition of the *Providence Journal* doesn't support that contention.

Instead, the article mentions the condemned housing, the mills that are shuttered, the foreclosures, the transience, homelessness, and fifteen-percent unemployment rate that are clearly evident if you spend time in the city and walk the streets and talk to the people.

The 2000 census described the racial makeup of the city as being 37.16 percent white, 5.82 percent African American, 0.57 percent Native American, 0.68 percent Asian, 0.04 percent Pacific Islander, 28.35 percent from other races, and 7.38 percent from two or more races. Latino was a significant percent of the population; however, in the intervening ten years this population has grown incrementally and doesn't include undocumented Latino immigrants.

Ziner's article describes the fear that has been generated throughout the city as the 2010 census approaches. It mentions Governor Carcieri's executive order cracking down on illegal immigration, and the immigration raids in factories in nearby Fall River and New Bedford that have "heightened anxieties, including within mixed-status families of illegal and legal immigrants."

The fear has state and census officials worried, since it is felt that there are many Latinos who will not participate in the 2010 census because, as explained by one man, "They don't trust the government anymore, and they feel threatened," in spite of explanations by immigration officials that the census is just a count and has nothing to do with illegal immigration.

At stake, of course, is a possible undercount that will have repercussions for a decade. As one state representative put it, an undercount could mean "people not getting food stamps, health care, enough money for education—everything would be cut."

For example, the 2000 census reported a population of 18,928 residents in a city with a median age of forty-seven, the majority of those residents being Latinos, and sixty-five percent of the residents speaking a language other than English in the home.

The truth is, nobody knows exactly how many people live in Central Falls. What we do know is that the 2000 figures are not accurate. The city's chief of police believes that there are over twenty-five thousand residents in the city, acknowledging that many are undocumented immigrants.

The city has an interesting past. Located five miles north of Providence in an area of slightly over one square mile, at one point it was the most densely populated city in the country. Originally a village in the town of Smithfield, it took its name from a waterfall on the nearby Blackstone River.

When Smithfield was divided into six smaller towns in 1871, the small Central Falls village was included in the town of Lincoln. Not until 1892 was Central Falls incorporated as a city.

Like other towns in the Blackstone Valley, Central Falls grew rapidly and evolved into a manufacturing center dominated by several large textile mills. The mills attracted immigrant workers who joined the French Canadians, Scots, and Irish who had settled in the city before the new influx of Poles, English, Syrians, Portuguese, Cape Verdeans, and Azoreans.

The workforce lived in three- or four-story tenements, with some families residing in small cold-water flats to save money. The crowded city saw several ethnic enclaves emerge, invariably revolving around a parish church or synagogue. Early on, the city established its identity as a community with rich ethnic diversity and a haven for blue-collar workers and their families.

However, by the early 1960s, most of the major factories were gone, creating a devastating effect on the city. The inexpensive housing and properties began to change hands. In an effort to survive, the remaining mill owners began recruiting some skilled loom fixers from Colombia to work in their mills.

Lured by cheap housing and jobs, the families, friends, and neighbors of this first contingent of Colombian workers migrated to the city in the 1970s and 1980s. Dominicans, Hondurans, Mexicans, Guatemalans, Puerto Ricans, and other Hispanic groups then joined the Colombians. The problem of absentee landlords and the lack of jobs emerged, and the rate of poverty climbed.

Today the city continues to be a potpourri of ethnic groups. The population grew by seven percent in the 1990s, the second-highest growth rate in a state whose overall population had declined.

The large majority of inhabitants are now Latino, a population that is very diverse and that has great variability in terms of countries of birth, primary language skills, and educational level.

As reported by Karen Ziner, if you walk down the three major roadways and commercial zones that bisect the city, "you will notice a bustle of activity with people speaking English, Spanish, Creole, K'iche, or Portuguese. You will see Colombian, Dominican, and other ethnic restaurants and businesses and Spanish-language papers on the newsstands.

"If you look down the narrow one-way streets, you will see spas, bars, and convenience stores scattered in the neighborhood and clusters of small children playing on the sidewalks, reminding us that this is a young city."

After realizing a small economic resurgence in the late 1990s, the city has been hit hard by the current recession, and it is difficult to believe that Central Falls is "a city with a bright future."

Recent indicators of poverty in Central Falls suggest that the living conditions for Latinos have worsened in recent years. For example, the food stamp program participation rate is at an all-time high, and the income-eligible school breakfast participation rate is up over ten percent since 2006.

Kids Count 2008 data shows that in Central Falls, over forty percent of children under the age of eighteen live in families below the poverty line, and slightly over forty percent of those children are considered to be living in extreme poverty. The last census indicated that the median family income was $26,844.

The challenges therefore are great. The promise for a better future will be determined by how well Latino children are being educated by the public schools. All students, parents, teachers, community organizations, state agencies, and churches must do their part.

State and federal legislators must step up to the plate and do more than just pass legislation that is not adequately funded. As the Hispanic population in this country continues to increase in the next decade, the challenges will be daunting.

It is within this context that chronically low-performing Central Falls High School began its organizational redesign, developing a more rigorous curriculum and better teaching practices. The ultimate goal, of course, was to improve student achievement as soon as possible, with some observable degree of sustainability.

CHAPTER 10

Central Falls High School Today

In September 2009, a group of Pennsylvania superintendents and assistant superintendents toured Central Falls High School. The visit was the culmination of a yearlong study program sponsored by Lehigh University in which each year a group of superintendents visits another state and listens to guest educators speak on a variety of educational issues.

The presentations are then followed by a site visit to a school district where the administrators can tour a school or schools, observe teachers in classrooms, and learn about new programs and initiatives.

The Pennsylvania administrators who toured Central Falls High School knew little about urban education or the challenges urban school administrators and teachers face in trying to close the achievement gap for minority students in the inner city. They had spent their professional careers in suburban districts.

Although several administrators had experience with diversity in their own districts, it was on a much smaller scale. They could only imagine what the urban school challenge might be, especially when they learned that forty-six percent of the Central Falls students were receiving either special education or English as a second language (ESL) services, and that the district had the highest number of children in the state under eighteen who lived in poverty.

You really had to wonder what they were thinking when they read that the high school graduation rate was less than fifty percent and that there were two teenage shootings in the past year that had occurred near the school, causing the Central Falls mayor to institute a nightly curfew throughout the city.

After the tour, the Pennsylvania educators met at Rhode Island College for a debriefing session. They were asked to write their reactions to what they had just witnessed at Central Falls High School.

Earlier in the week the group had listened to Superintendent Fran Gallo describe how the high school had just been reorganized into four themed academies: global studies, science and health arts, communication and teaching, and business and hospitality.

She mentioned that the ninth graders had been moved to their own separate building across town in an effort to provide intensive support and personalized instruction in order to ease their transition and enhance their chances for future success in high school.

Principal Liz Legault, a veteran Central Falls High School teacher and former middle school principal, had been appointed as the new high school principal the previous spring.

Liz provided a school overview to the Pennsylvania group prior to the school tour and explained that in the last three years, the high school had moved from a traditional model to more of a middle school design with teams (e.g., the ninth grade was a separate team, as were grades ten, eleven, and twelve), student advisories, block scheduling, common planning time for teachers, and a weekly staff development period.

She mentioned that special initiatives were now in place to improve school attendance, decrease tardiness, and reduce student suspensions and enthusiastically explained how she and her staff were determined to lower the dropout rate and increase the number of graduates who go on to further education.

The key, she said, "is to have the school become more meaningful and relevant to students and to encourage teachers to adopt a best-practice approach to teaching."

Liz reported cases where several veteran teachers were moving into interdisciplinary approaches to teaching and students were responding positively. The goal, she stressed, was for students to want to come to school each day and for them to gain the personal confidence they need for school success, knowing that the support and encouragement they also need is now in place.

She concluded her remarks by saying, "All of us—students, teachers, administrators, and parents—must raise our expectation levels for our students. We must get our kids to believe they can learn, and that what they learn will have meaning and value to them for the rest of their lives. If this attitude change occurs, the number of students who graduate and go on to college will significantly increase."

The feedback from the Pennsylvania administrators was quite positive, although it varied somewhat depending on the teachers they observed during their two hours in the school. The feedback was placed in four categories: General Comments, Administrative Leadership, Faculty, and Students. It was most revealing.

GENERAL COMMENTS

- "I expected the worst and it was not nearly as bad as the data would suggest."
- "The school is exciting!"
- "It's obvious that things are happening and will continue to happen if they stay the course."
- "Not as bad as I thought. An interesting application of middle school scheduling, student advisories, and teaming in a high school."
- "The ability of everyone to work under limited conditions, such as a lack of technology, is admirable."

ADMINISTRATIVE LEADERSHIP

- "Excellent leadership, top down—on the same page."
- "The high school under Liz Legault has a solid plan of action with logical, sequential steps to get there."
- "The passion and enthusiasm of the superintendent and principal is truly commendable."
- "The administrative team is very cohesive and has a focused path on restructuring the school."
- "The principal is on the right track. She has the determination, vision, and energy to change the culture and increase student achievement. It will be a steep climb, however."

FACULTY

- "More teachers need to be schooled in best-practice strategies."
- "The administrative staff is cohesive and focused; however, the rest of the staff needs to get on board."
- "The teachers I met were helpful and passionate about the new initiatives."
- "There was some really good teaching going on in the classrooms I observed."
- "I was impressed by students and administrators, but not nearly as impressed with the faculty aside from a couple of teachers I met."
- "Most teachers were enthusiastic and focused."

STUDENTS

- "The kids were wonderful. Very polite and well behaved in all classrooms."
- "The students were engaged and very respectful."
- "The students were delightful and very positive."
- "Students appear happy in their environment and want to be actively involved in their own education."

Although the Pennsylvania delegation viewed only a snapshot of the high school, their informal comments support some of the findings of the Commissioner's Review two years earlier. Although there were a lot of positive comments, there were still concerns about teaching practice and a hint that some teachers were not committed to supporting the new initiatives.

On the other hand, there was now a clear direction for change from the central office and the high school leadership, with a "cohesive and focused plan in place," as one of the visiting superintendents phrased it.

There were also signs that the passion and dedication of the superintendent and high school principal were beginning to "bear fruit" with teachers who had been disillusioned in the past with the turnover and instability of the school's leadership.

CHAPTER 11

An Agenda for Change

Two women have played major roles in putting in place a change strategy that has ignited teaching and learning at Central Falls High School during the past three years. The first is Anna Cano Morales, chair of the board of trustees and a member of the State Board of Regents for Elementary and Secondary Education.

Anna was born and raised in Central Falls, the daughter of Colombian immigrants who worked in the local textile mills. She is an articulate and active advocate for Latino families and their school-aged children, a person who has "walked the walk" and realizes what it takes for Latino students to succeed in school and in life.

She is compassionate, but she is also impatient with the slow progress being made in raising student achievement in Central Falls schools. She is a woman with a clear vision of what Central Falls High School can become: a model school of excellence; a place other urban schools will want to emulate.

Along with many others, she is determined to change the negative image of Central Falls and its schools, as well as to get the word out to the public that there are great things happening in the schools, and it will only get better in the next few years.

A woman of boundless energy and enthusiasm, Anna entered the Talent Development program while at the University of Rhode Island (URI), a program that provides academic support and personal assistance for undergraduate minority students prior to and during their enrollment in college.

Anna blossomed as a student, both academically and in leadership confidence. She currently is an associate vice president at the Rhode Island Foundation, a major philanthropic organization located in Providence, and sits on the URI Foundation Board, as well as on a variety of other boards and committees whose purpose is to advance the cause and influence of Rhode Island's growing Latino population.

One of Anna's and the board of trustees' best decisions was to appoint Fran Gallo as school superintendent in 2007. Fran had an impressive track record of leadership success in school reform initiatives while serving as deputy superintendent in Providence.

A petite, energetic woman with a passion for the underserved, Fran is the daughter of first-generation Italian immigrant parents, and through her own humble upbringing has developed an understanding and appreciation of the struggles low-income families face.

Fran's first challenge was to take the recommended partnership between URI and Central Falls High School and, as she explains, "put the words on the pages into action."

In her first year, she reorganized the central office staff, causing many longtime administrators to leave the district. She replaced them with successful urban school educators she knew or had previously worked with who shared her vision and philosophy and weren't reluctant to challenge the status quo.

The high school administrative team was completely replaced and department heads were eliminated when the school was reorganized with grade-level teams and upper-school academies in 2009.

Her goal was to make the high school a welcoming place where students would want to come each day—a place that served students and not adults; a place where teachers were personally and professionally committed to their students and open to making the changes and adaptations required. She wanted students to look beyond high school and aspire to higher career goals and service to their community.

Fran is a bold leader who is willing to take risks and doesn't shy away from controversy. When she sees an opportunity to improve the status quo, she grabs it.

For example, the Community School, a local charter school in Central Falls that enrolls a number of Central Falls youngsters, was getting amazing results in increasing student reading achievement.

Fran was quoted in the state paper saying, "What is it? They have the same demographics as us. Their parents are our parents. They don't turn away special education students."

Because she was impressed with the Community School's reading strategies, she formed an unprecedented partnership with the charter school and asked them to train her elementary school teachers. This training involved Community School instructional coaches sharing practical tactics, teacher to teacher, in real urban classrooms.

After a one-year pilot program showed significant gains at or above the national benchmark, the training was expanded to all of the city's elementary schools and teachers.

Fran realizes that in many cases it might be too late to help students arriving in grade nine with a record of school failure, and only elementary-level literacy and math skills. The need to keep the door open, however, is very important, and the role of the urban school district and other agencies in establishing effective adult education programs to serve this population is paramount.

Fran also believes that a solid foundation in math and literacy must be built in the early grades. She explained that success for urban kids at all levels "is about creating a welcoming environment and fidelity to a curriculum. It's about teaching from early in the morning until late at night and teaching to high standards. And it's about using your team to pull in a tight circle around your students."

The recent improved achievement results for Central Falls elementary students is not a surprise and bodes well for those students who will later proceed to the middle and high schools, but Fran knows that it is much harder to maintain that level of success in the middle and high schools, especially with the constant turnover of students.

Balancing accountability, dwindling funds, and ever-changing sets of standards and requirements on the more labor-intensive and costly secondary level makes it difficult to provide the type of individual and small-group instruction new students like English-language learners need. Fran realizes that bold leadership on her part is necessary if sustainable change is to occur.

The teacher union leadership, however, does not buy all of Fran's initiatives. Although they feel they have been cooperative and supportive of many of the recent changes, the major union priority is to protect their detailed and at times inflexible contract, even when the grassroots membership expresses a willingness to change.

As one Pennsylvania superintendent put it, "The teachers, especially the union leadership, need to get on or get off the reform ship as it leaves the harbor."

Fran realizes that the union leadership has a role to play; however, she often sees that role inhibiting needed change and improvement. She explains, "Many times the union leadership's opposition to my initiatives is not in the best interests of students. In those cases, I go ahead and do them anyway. If they want to file grievances let them."

Fran truly is a remarkably strong, passionate leader and an advocate for underserved students. Her small size and quiet demeanor are deceptive and belie her mental toughness and tenacity of purpose. She clearly will not be deterred. The dismal achievement statistics of Latino students in her school district cannot be denied. The status quo is simply not acceptable, nor should it be.

CHAPTER 12

The URI–Central Falls
High School Partnership

Prior to forming a formal partnership with URI, Central Falls High School was undergoing change based upon new state graduation requirements, and recommendations contained in a "correction plan" that was jointly developed by the school and the Rhode Island State Department of Education (RIDE).

The recommendations followed reviews conducted by the commissioner of education, in which evaluations of the changes were made and progress toward improvement was determined.

The changes implemented by the school in the last three years follow a popular model that calls for smaller learning communities for students through the formation of grade-level teams and career academies; block scheduling that provides increased time for learning; common planning time for teachers where students are the focus; individualized learning plans for all students; and a core requirement of college preparatory courses for all students.

Other changes were the introduction of student advisory programs, which provide more personalized settings where teachers can support individual students and rescue them if necessary; increased time for more embedded professional training of teachers; and, as mentioned previously, a separate freshman program that helps students successfully negotiate the transition from middle school to high school. Many of these new initiatives were underway before Fran Gallo arrived in Central Falls.

The URI–Central Falls High School Academy project has helped transform the high school by better shaping past changes, creating new external and internal programs, and providing new capital, both financial and human. For example, a one-million-dollar, three-year grant by the Rhode Island Foundation provided critically needed resources in supporting the new partnership.

The university assigned Abu Bakr, executive assistant to the URI president, and Ron DiOrio, a URI education professor, to the high school, representing a significant resource investment. Both gentlemen have played key roles as university liaisons and members of the Partnership Governance Board, a representative group that oversees high school reform and makes commendations and recommendations on progress or lack thereof toward targeted reform goals.

Currently the group is evaluating the implementation of the junior- and senior-year career academies in hospitality, the arts, health, global studies, communication and teaching, and business, with the major purpose being to support the work of the academies and to make them more effective.

During the past three years, the partnership, supported by a Rhode Island Foundation grant, has had an impact in several areas through initiatives such as a dual-enrollment program initiated by URI that allows high school students to earn college credit, and the hiring of an increased number of outreach workers and home liaisons, which has enhanced family and community engagement.

One of the more successful partnership initiatives was the creation of an academic support center (called the Academic Enhancement Center, or AEC) equipped with new technology. One full-time professional and a number of undergraduate tutors from URI staff the center. A summer program for students who are demonstrating academic proficiency, as well as one for those students who are below proficiency, is also part of the Academic Enhancement Center's program.

The partnership also created a summer math program for eighth-grade students who failed math and were in jeopardy of being retained at the middle school, and established the TALL (Transition Through Arts Literacy Learning) University Program, a program that is designed to improve literacy through the arts and is funded by the foundation grant.

Preliminary results of the partnership and other reform initiatives over the past three years have been encouraging. The high school now has full accreditation, and state assessment scores have increased eleven percent in reading and ten percent in math.

Although student achievement scores are still relatively very low, these small signs of progress are encouraging. The high school has also passed the two Commissioner Reviews, in which it was cited for three model practices: the integration of the student advisory program into the school culture; the individual learning plans that were embraced by the student body; and the successful implementation of common planning time.

A more comprehensive evaluation of high school reform during the past two years is currently being conducted by Brown University's Education Alliance. Preliminary findings are encouraging, with students expressing high satisfaction with the URI-related ventures, especially the assistance provided by the Academic Enhancement Center, the literacy and math support programs, and the student advisory program.

Teacher feedback has been positive regarding common planning time, the assistance provided by the home-school liaisons and outreach workers, and the additional laptops and software now available in the AEC. The full evaluation report is expected in late 2010.

CHAPTER 13

A Severe Bump in the Road

On February 9, 2010, the Central Falls High School auditorium was packed with teachers, students, alumni, and parents. Police were standing at the doorways, and television reporters and photographers were meandering about trying to get the best view. It was standing room only. Because of fire codes, a crowd of people was not let into the auditorium but stood outside the school discussing what was about to occur inside.

The auditorium balcony was teeming with students carrying signs telling teachers "We Will Fight for You!" Parents and teachers were waving homemade signs at the officials on the stage that said "Shame on You!" and "Negotiate Don't Terminate!"

One could feel the tension in the room and the growing hostility toward the superintendent of schools, members of the board of trustees, and building administrators, who were quietly sitting behind long tables, adjusting their microphones as they prepared to address the board agenda.

Those in attendance were expecting the board to vote to terminate all members of the high school faculty. The agenda indicated that the superintendent would be recommending the "reconstitution of the high school and termination and/or nonrenewal of staff."

Superintendent Gallo had notified the union leadership that such action was pending. Teachers were naturally upset, and things had recently gotten ugly when students, parents, and alumni learned of the pending action. Fear, misinformation, and rumor had spread through the community like wildfire via a Facebook posting in the days before the meeting.

Prior to the meeting, teachers conducted a candlelight vigil and marched from the nearby middle school to the high school auditorium. Suddenly the auditorium chatter and constant hum ended. A historic meeting was about to begin.

Superintendent Gallo opened the meeting and moved quickly to the termination agenda item. She indicated that a vote would not be taken at this meeting, but at the next February board meeting, unless an agreement with the teachers' union to accept a school reform plan that called for more dramatic transformation of the school in "deeper ways than we have been doing" was reached within the next three days.

She intimated that the union had refused to accept a revised school reform plan, and this refusal would automatically lead to a state take-over of the school and most likely the termination of up to fifty percent or even the entire school staff.

Gallo explained that she was forced to take the termination action because she had been notified by State Commissioner of Education Deborah Gist that the high school, in spite of progressive state inter-vention assistance and recent achievement gains through reform efforts in all Central Falls schools, had failed to meet state targets in student achievement for the seventh year in a row.

As a Title I school with a forty-eight percent graduation rate, a fifty-five percent proficiency in reading and literacy, and a seven percent proficiency in math, the high school fell into the lowest five percent of low-performing schools in the state and therefore had been designated as one of the "persistently lowest achieving schools."

The new reform directive can be traced to the U.S. Department of Education mandate and Arne Duncan, the new Secretary of Educa-tion, who is pushing the Chicago model he used while superintendent in that city as a method to turn around chronically low-performing urban schools.

Commissioner Gist had quickly followed his directive and developed a state intervention protocol that called for the selected low-achieving schools to take one of the following actions: (1) close the school, (2) replace the principal if she or he has been in that role for more than two years, increase the length of the instructional school day, and change instructional practices—an option called "the transformational model," (3) hire a charter school or outside management company to run the school, or (4) implement the so-called turn-around model, where the principal is replaced and no more than fifty percent of the staff can be rehired.

The local school district had the initial opportunity to accept any one of the four options and was required to develop a school plan and present it to the commissioner for acceptance. Failure to reach local agreement to select a plan and/or the unsuccessful implementation of the eventual plan would trigger a reconstitution action to be determined by the state.

At the meeting, Superintendent Gallo outlined the planning process she had followed in the past six months, discussing the work that had been done by a stakeholder group that included the union leaders along with other representative groups.

She explained that the feedback received from the stakeholders indicated that the transformational model "held the most promise and opportunity for our students and teachers." All agreed that it was clearly the best fit and coincided with the changes and work the school had already done in seeking future Race to the Top and Title I School Improvement funding.

Gallo indicated that four new school reform models currently in place throughout the country were being considered for the high school, and site visits to schools with these models in place had already been completed. She expressed disappointment that after all this activity and planning, the union was still not on board with the transformation model plan.

She explained that the union was objecting to the required preconditions of the model that called for extending the school day by twenty-five minutes; a teacher commitment of one hour of weekly tutoring outside the school day; paid professional development for two weeks outside the typical school calendar; agreement to meet ninety minutes each week to look at student work and successful professional practices, assess data, and plan units of study; the use of third-party evaluators to evaluate all high school teachers; and finally, eating lunch with students once per week.

She concluded her overview by explaining that she was required to notify the commissioner that she could not bring about a resolution that would get us to the transformational model.

She then read a letter she had written and given to the union president, Jane Sessums, a few minutes before the board meeting. The letter stated that she was notifying the commissioner that the union was rejecting the transformational model under the conditions outlined. She indicated that she had to deliver the letter to the commissioner within the next three days.

Anna Cano Morales, chair of the trustees, then asked for public comments. What transpired next was an orchestrated series of statements from state and local union leaders. Although they too favored the transformational model and were represented on the stakeholder committee, they felt excluded in determining the specifics of the model and wanted more details on the reform models currently being considered. They were particularly critical of the specific preconditions as outlined by Gallo.

They asked the superintendent to sit down with the union and follow a bargaining process in determining the list of preconditions, in order to avoid being placed in what they felt was a "take it or leave it" situation.

The state president of the American Federation of Teachers (AFT), Marcia Reeback, used strong language in her remarks. She stated that there was a "toxic" relationship between the administration and faculty unlike anything she had ever seen. She accused Superintendent Gallo of using teacher jobs as a way of holding seventy-four teachers hostage, and also of increasing their workload by fifteen percent without compensation.

Reeback pointed to the badges teachers were wearing that said "Do things with us, not to us." She concluded by saying, "The union is willing to work with you to reach a reasonable agreement, but it is a two-way street. If you continue to pursue this action by terminating all the teachers at the high school, it will show you for what you are."

Jane Sessums, president of the Central Falls Teacher's Union, and Jim Parisi, an AFT executive, stated that they "want to be at the table" and objected to the way Gallo had proceeded using such a short timeline.

Sessums complained about receiving Gallo's letter at the last moment and informed the crowd that no teacher is "in correction" as a result of recent teacher evaluations conducted by high school administrators. She called using outside evaluators after teachers receive termination notices a "bit backwards." When each union official completed their remarks, they received loud standing ovations from the overflow crowd.

One longtime teacher and union advocate who called himself the faculty "troublemaker" grabbed the microphone. In an angry, passionate tone, he told the superintendent and board how they were destroying his school family and tearing the heart out of every Central Falls student, teacher, and parent.

He claimed that the superintendent had upset him greatly when she told him that "history is dead now, this is a new time." He promised to fight for what is right and do whatever it takes to stop what he termed "a distasteful action."

Several students read poems praising their teachers, while others gave testimony about how the teachers stay after school helping them, use their own money for school expenses, act as caring mentors, and make up an important part of one big school family.

One student said, "They are more than teachers, they are our friends."

Another said, "We are the Warriors, we are special in our own way. If you destroy our family, I won't like you." This young man was an infamous discipline problem, and his testimony was a surprise. Although a difficult student, he was a talented artist and after his remarks, he held up two intricate and colorful posters honoring his teachers, then returned to his seat showered with thunderous applause.

Several students cried openly and had difficulty finishing their remarks. They spoke of how important certain teachers were in their lives and how they "appreciated all that they do for us."

A particularly poignant moment occurred when a young female special education student came to the microphone and froze. She attempted to restart her remarks several times, but each time froze after repeating her first sentence. She then stood quietly at the microphone as a silence descended over the audience. Her teacher then came to her rescue and escorted her back to her seat as everyone in the audience clapped for what seemed like several minutes.

For those people out of the loop who thought progress was finally occurring at the school, the present crisis was a surprise. They were caught off guard. The positive impact of the URI partnership was evident, test scores were creeping upward, school attendance was significantly better, and a host of organizational changes, such as the formation of the new career academies, were underway.

Then along came the federal government and a new state commissioner and another degrading designation of the high school as a "persistently lowest-achieving school" that was now facing possible reconstitution by the state. It was upsetting to students and teachers. It just didn't seem fair.

One has to sympathize with the high school students and those dedicated, "high-performing teachers" on the faculty who give so much of themselves every day while facing the special challenges of teaching in a high-poverty urban school.

You can understand their sense of betrayal and outrage. Even if they were the most qualified and effective teachers in the school, they could be out of a job, with their lives disrupted and all their good work done in vain. Their chances of being rehired would now mainly be determined by a still undefined outside evaluation process developed in conjunction with the state. This was not a comforting thought.

Some people were claiming that past school-level administrators, fearing union opposition and the loss of faculty support, had significantly contributed to the problem by giving mediocre teachers satisfactory evaluations. It was difficult to believe that there weren't any teachers on a correction plan, but it was confirmed that there were none.

The assumption being made is that if talented urban teachers could replace the mediocre ones, the high school would move ahead at greater speed. It's difficult to disagree with that, especially if the "new blood" is sufficient enough to change the chemistry and culture of the school.

However, this is a big "if" because of the variables that are involved. The school runs the risk of losing some of its master teachers, who are now disillusioned and may not even want to be rehired. They have been caught in the crossfire with their reputations tarnished and their job security threatened. Losing some of its top teachers to other districts would set the school back.

The other variable is replacing those teachers who are not rehired. Is there a ready supply of exceptional urban teachers available who want to work in such a volatile situation as Central Falls High School? Unlikely, unless you can offer financial incentives to attract proven, highly qualified urban teachers.

One's heart goes out to the students as well. They too are caught in the middle. Many have bonded with a core of truly dedicated teachers who have made a difference in their lives. Given the conditions in which they live, this is not to be taken lightly.

The students featured in this book have identified teachers whom they admire and appreciate for what they have done for them, both on a personal and on an academic level. They explain that forming these relationships was crucial to their school success.

However, in spite of some modest improvements, one can understand why there is a call for deeper change in the high school. After years of state corrective intervention and assistance, the high dropout rate and the low student achievement results on state assessment tests are still unacceptable. Both sides in this dispute agree on that.

The apparent failure of the teachers' union to accept the transformational model and avoid the termination of high school teachers was therefore particularly puzzling. Here was an opportunity to attack the problem in an aggressive way and prove that the current leadership and faculty were up to the task.

Was it simply an issue of getting more money for extra time and resistance to third party evaluation? Was this a political power play with teachers and students as pawns? Only those behind closed doors know the real answers to those questions.

At the board meeting, the superintendent and board members respectfully took public comments but knew it was not the time or place for counter arguments. For example, no one got up and challenged the union's position or talked about the fact that for seven years, the high school has been a low-performing school and still has a graduation rate below fifty percent.

The union points to ways they have cooperated in the change initiative; however, their flood of petty grievances and their resistance to major changes in the status quo have diverted attention away from the real crisis at hand and created doubt that the current faculty has the wherewithal to turn the school around.

This lack of cooperation generates distrust between administrators and teachers and contributes to the toxicity that Marcia Reeback alluded to in her remarks. Toxicity, however, is a two-way street, and unquestionably, powerful teacher unions in Rhode Island generate more than their share of toxicity.

The union leadership has to be held accountable, too, because it has had distrustful relationships with a number of building and central administrators during the past seven years, with most of those administrators having been forced to leave the district voluntarily or involuntarily.

Unlike the national AFT leadership, which recently expressed a willingness to consider Washington's school reform agenda, both the state and local AFT leadership in Central Falls refuse to budge from their traditional hard-line labor positions. As one former school administrator remarked, "It may be a time for a change in union leadership if they are genuinely going to be part of the solution. A new vision is needed. This isn't 1955, it's 2010."

A local politician shared this opinion about unions: "Hey, that stuff going on in Central Falls comes with the thankless job of being a school superintendent in a small state where strong, politically connected unions have had their own way far too long.

"They give lip service to reform, but their real agenda is to protect and please their membership and support their locals. Layoffs or terminations or asking them to drop their seniority rights will naturally raise hell in their ranks. You are asking them to give up their power and control in order to better serve kids in need. Give me a break, this is Rhode Island! If you think they are going to change, you are whistling in the dark and no one's listening."

This cynicism is not helpful. One would like to think that with the national AFT's recent openness to the national change agenda, a new era of cooperation between school unions and management might be emerging in Rhode Island and Central Falls. However, the ugly dispute between the union and administration raises serious doubts about that happening. Hopefully, this thorny problem can be solved without terminating teachers, especially the talented ones.

It was interesting to note that at the board meeting, no one made public comments about students not graduating, students not learning at the rate and level they should, students dropping out at an alarming rate, and too many students letting opportunities pass them by.

Yes, teachers are nurturing, caring friends, and the common bonds of friendship and support fill voids left by the impoverished environment in which many of these students live. This is critically important, but this is all most of the students really see.

The students spoke in support of their school and their special friends, their teachers. They showed tremendous school pride as they chanted, "We Are the Warriors!" However, what about the other fifty percent of the kids who weren't there because they had dropped by the wayside? Where are those warriors today?

High school teachers claim that they were the only constant in the high school and that the instability caused by the frequent turnover of administrators contributed to low student achievement. However, there is one major difference. If an administrator failed, he or she was replaced and a more effective leader was sought, while mediocre teachers remained, protected by their tenure and their union.

A case can be made that ineffective administrators and ineffective teachers should both be replaced if student achievement is to increase. This, of course, has not been the case at Central Falls High School. It is the administrators who have been shown the door.

But one teacher did make an interesting point. During the state intervention period, when the school was under a correction plan with changing principals and superintendents, there was always some new program or direction that teachers were asked to embrace through either a new mandate from the state or by a favored program introduced by new school or central office administrators.

This veteran teacher said this influx of new ideas and programs, many later discarded, created a "new flavor of the month" situation that led to faculty cynicism. He said one exception was the URI–Central Falls High School partnership, where careful and transparent planning and implementation were well done and well communicated, with follow-through by URI when it committed the necessary resources and long-range on-site assistance.

He felt that the student and teacher benefits and services provided by the partnership were becoming increasingly apparent as the project embedded itself more deeply into the fabric of the school.

Another thing that was upsetting many taxpayers was hearing that teachers wanted extra money for extending the school day by twenty-five minutes. Students indicated that they constantly saw many of their teachers staying after school, helping students, sometimes hours after school ended.

People were asking why, at this point in time, teachers wanted extra pay in their base salary for extending the school day by just twenty-five minutes when they already received extra pay for time spent after school and beyond the school calendar year, and, as many claim, they already stayed after school helping students without compensation.

The average teacher in Central Falls is currently making between $72,000 to $78,000 a year and now allegedly wants extra money for the extension of the school day. With a state school aid shortfall in the midst of the largest state fiscal crisis in recent memory, such a demand does not sit well with the general public and is fodder for the teacher bashers.

Rhode Island is in economic stagnation, near the top of national unemployment charts and facing a budget shortfall this year and a pro-jected deficit of four hundred million dollars for the next fiscal year. It is understandable why there is little public support for increased teacher pay when so many people are unemployed and others are just trying to hold on to their present jobs.

The proposal for teacher professional time outside the school day and school calendar will pay teachers $3400 more per year, or thirty dollars per hour, which is stipulated in the current contract. The media reported that the union now wanted ninety dollars per hour.

Fran Gallo was now giving the union two more days to come on board. She insisted that reconstitution was not her first choice, but she was left no other choice because of the union's recalcitrance. She was also facing a February 22 termination notice deadline established by state law.

She explained her reasons for her tough stance in an article published in the *Providence Journal* the day after the board meeting. "We have a graduation rate of forty-eight percent. I have nineteen-year-olds in class with fourteen-year-olds. It's the middle of the school year and fifty percent of the high school students are failing their classes. We have to meet the students where they are, and bring them up and lift the bar."

Hopefully, this crisis will be averted and cooler heads will prevail. The stakes are very high, and the bold shake-up and somewhat punitive initiatives proposed by the federal government and the state could backfire, particularly in a time of shrinking resources.

On the other hand, such conflicts also open up new opportunities. Let's pray that the current momentum and positive changes that have taken place in the past four years will not be lost, but built upon as the change equation gets reformulated once again.

CHAPTER 14

Central Falls Students

Every time a young person is shot and killed on the streets of an inner city, the local high school's reputation worsens. This is true in Central Falls even if the teenager was not currently enrolled in the school.

The public perception is that the high school must be a dangerous place; a place with unruly students, large-scale student suspensions, and resource officers patrolling the corridors with revolvers on their hips, ready to break up ugly fights on a moment's notice. (Note that most high schools, urban and suburban, now hire resource officers.)

Central Falls High School naturally suffers from this misguided perception because there is a higher rate of crime in Central Falls than in other parts of the state. The small city is wedged between Pawtucket and Providence, two major cities. Invariably, crimes related to gang conflicts and drugs in those cities spill over to the Central Falls neighborhoods.

As previously reported, visitors to the high school are surprised when they observe an orderly school environment and students who are respectful, polite, and well behaved. Those who visit and observe and talk to the students call them "wonderful kids," and they are, in spite of the obstacles they must overcome.

Although most of them are from families with limited means, they are similar to their suburban counterparts in many ways. Obviously, there are more students from poor families where the heads of the household are single parents, working multiple jobs and suffering from the residual fallout created by poverty, limited English proficiency, and low educational levels.

But just like suburban parents, Latino parents love their children dearly and want them to succeed and have a better life than they have had. Having the time and energy to be involved in their child's education is another matter.

Similar to suburban students, Central Falls students look forward to their school proms, express pride in the success of their athletic teams and state-champion chess team, work part-time jobs to help support their families, are fiercely loyal to their friends, enjoy kibitzing with their favorite teachers, look forward to getting their driver's license and a car someday, and engage in adolescent courtships and all that activity entails.

They also have immense pride in their school and become defensive when incidents happen in the city that negatively reflect the image of their school. They insist that their school is not a "jungle," in spite of what may be going on outside its walls.

Their school is a safe and caring community, a learning community that is trying hard to get better results, a community that is serious about reform and expending considerable energy and resources to change the status quo and better serve its students.

MAEROFF AND SUCCESSFUL URBAN STUDENTS

Fran Gallo mentioned that she could identify for me some recent graduates who not only beat the odds, but also excelled in the classroom or in leadership roles—students who were class leaders, overcame adversity, or somehow rose to the top of their class academically. They had to be graduates of the class of 2009 and currently freshmen in college. It wasn't necessary for all of them to be Latino.

An emphasis was placed on finding students who had actually profited from their four years at the high school. Answers to key questions were sought. Why did they succeed when so many others failed? What motivated them? Did they have unique support systems composed of encouraging parents and teachers who held high expectations for them and believed in them?

More importantly, how did they avoid the pitfalls that had swallowed up so many of their classmates in a class with only a forty-eight percent graduation rate? How did they feel about the possibility that some of their teachers might lose their jobs? It was important to get to know these students well and get their answers to these questions and others in order to share the reasons for their success with other Central Falls students and families.

At the same time, the students had to be representative of the diversity of the student body and reflective of the demographic profile of families in Central Falls. It would not be easy finding students who met all these requirements.

There was another key question that needed answering by the students. It related to a book by Gene Maeroff of Columbia University titled *Altered Destinies: Making Life Better for School Children*, in which he called the crisis of low-performing urban high schools "an embarrassment of America."

His words stung because before the current teacher firing controversy, Central Falls was not considered an embarrassment, but a school on the move. Stereotyping all inner-city high schools as "embarrassing" sounded counterproductive and was an unfair knock at the dedicated urban teachers and school leaders who labor daily with the enormous challenges of teaching poor inner-city minority youth.

On the other hand, Maeroff could point to many urban high schools throughout the country that were going nowhere—schools that were perpetuating mediocrity rather than attacking the problem head-on in new, dramatic, and innovative ways.

Maeroff also said another thing that really was bothersome. His quote read, "The highest-achieving students in too many urban high schools are simply doing the minimum, performing at grade level."

It was difficult believing that was the case at Central Falls High School. The students interviewed in this book were asked to react to Maeroff's statement—a statement that implies they were slipping by and were products of a mediocre education due to a watered-down curriculum.

The true test, of course, is whether the students were adequately prepared for the challenges of higher education and will succeed academically and actually graduate from college.

It should be noted that the low college persistence and completion rates for Latino students are a matter of record, and too many are dropping out of college after a year or two. However, many of the drop-outs are from community colleges where students leave periodically to work full time and revert to part-time student status, or leave school for economic reasons but return in later years to complete their degrees. This data is hard to track, but the persistence problem can't be denied.

The school achievers featured in this book are all attending four-year colleges full time, but still work part time. Although the probability of their graduating on time with a college degree is high, there is no guarantee, especially for one student who needed additional assistance in high school in literacy and attended a college preparedness summer program before being accepted as a full-time college student.

The plan was to interview each student and follow them through their first year of college. It was also necessary to receive feedback from their parents, teachers, siblings, and friends in order to more fully understand the journey, both personally and educationally, taken by these young people during the first eighteen years of their lives.

THE FOUR STUDENTS

The three recommended students were Theresa Agonia, Bryant Estrada, and George Carle. A fourth student, Guillermo Ronquillo, was added later at the recommendation of Bryant Estrada.

Theresa Agonia is an attractive, effervescent young lady whose parents emigrated from the Minho Province in Portugal in the late 1970s. Born in 1991, she is the youngest of three children. Her father ran a successful small construction company but died of bile duct cancer at the age of fifty-seven when she was a junior in high school.

Theresa had a special relationship with her dad and greatly admired him and the work ethic that led to his success as a businessman. His loss was a devastating blow to her and created financial and legal problems for her family.

Bryant Estrada is the youngest child of immigrant Colombian parents. An older sister is currently a student at the University of Rhode Island, Providence campus. Bryant battled epilepsy most of his life, but now considers himself a mild epileptic since medication keeps his condition under control most of the time. He had a small recurrence during the stressful college application period in his senior year.

The third student, George Carle, is the son of a Puerto Rican single mom who had a troubled and violent past, but has turned her life around in recent years. His mother, Rosa Rosado, was born in a tough Providence neighborhood where violence and drugs were a way of life.

In addition to George, Rosa has two younger sons who are currently students at the high school. A soft-spoken and humble young man, George is her eldest child and a celebrated high school athlete who is now chasing his dream of playing college basketball and getting his college degree.

Theresa and Bryant were born in Central Falls and attended the local schools from kindergarten through their high school graduation in 2009. George's situation was much different, since his mother had moved several times while her children were small. As a result, George attended a variety of schools in other communities before his mother permanently settled in Central Falls.

The three students were excellent examples of "school achievers" in a low-performing inner-city high school, but something was missing. What was needed was a non-English-speaking student who had immigrated to Rhode Island with his family after beginning school in his native country and eventually graduated from Central Falls High School in 2009.

Bryant recommended Guillermo Ronquillo, a young man who ended up as class salutatorian, finishing just behind the class valedictorian, who just happened to be Bryant Estrada. Bryant was impressed with how quickly Guillermo had mastered English, both spoken and written, and had become an honors student. They became fast friends and inspired each other to work harder in their reach for academic excellence.

Guillermo is the older of two boys whose parents left El Salvador in 1999 when the father suffered a major financial setback. He entered the fourth grade in the neighboring city of Pawtucket knowing only a couple of words of English.

He entered Central Falls High School as a ninth grader in 2006 when his family bought a house in the city. In his four years in high school, he blossomed into an exceptional student in spite of a rocky start in his first semester.

Although the four students are different, they are similar in one important aspect. They are survivors. Their stories provide details on how they overcame personal adversity and managed to achieve school success. Hopefully, new insights into what it took for these students to gain the inner confidence, personal motivation, and will to set and achieve lofty goals will be evident.

The four student narratives are meant to provide inspiration and motivation to other students and their parents, helping them carve an educational path that will result in increased academic success and ultimately a brighter future for this generation of Central Falls students and the generations to come.

CHAPTER 15

Theresa Agonia—Overcoming Adversity

Theresa and her mother, Fernanda, were sitting at the dining room table. Both women were weeping. Silence then filled the room, allowing time for both of them to regain their composure.

In her broken English, Fernanda said, "It's not fair to fire all the teachers. They have done so much for Theresa. It's not their fault that the students don't want to do well in school."

Wiping tears from her beautiful brown eyes, Theresa spoke softly, "When my Dad got sick and died, no one knows how certain teachers took me under their wing. They gave me the support I desperately needed and contributed to my self-confidence. They were there when I needed them."

The youngest of three children, Theresa adored her father and marveled that with only a fourth-grade education he had become a highly popular and successful building contractor. As the youngest, Theresa was "daddy's little girl." Tall, slender, and striking, with a winning smile and bubbling personality, she was a finalist in the Miss Rhode Island Teen Pageant when she learned that her dad had bile duct cancer.

She attended Portuguese school four hours per week for nine years, and with her family was active in the Portuguese community. She particularly enjoyed dancing, having performed with the Salsa and Rancho Folk Dancing groups for nine years. She was one busy young lady.

But seeing her dad suffer and unable to work during her first two years of high school was hard for Theresa. She had difficulty concentrating on her studies and found herself preoccupied with her dad's deteriorating condition.

Her dad eventually died at the age of fifty-seven in the middle of her junior year, and Theresa speaks sadly about the loss of her loving dad.

"He never got to see me in my senior prom dress or being crowned Miss Portugal Rhode Island or getting accepted into college. He was an incredible man and father and well thought of in the community. There were over one thousand people at his funeral. He was so admired and well respected.

"I want to be like him. When he died I felt empty. He was my inspiration. He is not physically with me now, but he lives on in my heart."

During her ordeal, Theresa reached out to her teachers. "They were there for me, especially my English teachers, Michael Occhi and Deloris Grant."

Theresa was especially close to Michael Occhi, who taught her in class and also worked with her as the faculty advisor when she was editor of the senior yearbook.

Theresa said Michael was a memorable character, one of those teachers you never forget. He coached the chess team and led them to the state championship. He loved Emily Dickinson and helped finance yearly trips to her birthplace, where students recited her poetry at her grave. He took his class to Salem when they read literature about the witch trials.

Michael loved the Beatles and had a nickname for everyone. He played guitar and made students sing sea ballads when they read *Moby Dick*. He was totally devoted to Central Falls students and would maintain contact and help them with life's struggles years after they left high school.

Michael was demanding and persuasive, and he challenged students and administrators. One student was quoted as saying, "He could make you mad because he would get on you to do your work, to read, to write, but he would go out of his way to help students."

Every year, Michael visited the superintendent's office to get financial donations for the yearbook. On those occasions, he wore a herringbone sports jacket and a Christmas tie. It took him only a few minutes to get me to write him a check. He would have been a million-dollar salesman if he hadn't gone into teaching.

Theresa leaned heavily on Michael during her father's illness and after his death. Tragically, shortly after she graduated, Michael was killed by a drunk driver while driving a moped in his hometown. His death sent shock waves throughout the Central Falls community. Theresa was devastated. She and other students created a DVD celebrating his life that was played at Michael's funeral.

Weeks later, with her classmates and teachers, she helped organize a candlelight vigil in his honor. The school had suffered an incredible loss and Theresa had lost a dear friend and mentor.

Unfortunately, Theresa's personal adversity didn't end with the deaths of her dad and Michael Occhi.

Theresa's father had a will, but after his death, there was a dispute with his brothers over the house where Theresa's family had lived for years on the second floor, and where her grandmother had lived on the first floor.

Shortly after her father's death, his brothers asked Theresa's family to pay rent for the first time. These were the same brothers who had worked with him in the family business and at one time had lived on the third floor of the family tenement.

A nasty legal battle ensued. Theresa, her brother, sister, and mother refused to pay rent and decided to move to a house in nearby Cumberland while Theresa completed her senior year in Central Falls. The action by the brothers has created bad feelings and a split in the once close-knit family. As Theresa said, "When I lost my father, I lost most of his side of the family too."

In Cumberland, finances were tight for the Agonia family. Theresa, her mother, brother, and sister pooled their money to meet expenses. Theresa had worked part time for Kentucky Fried Chicken (KFC) throughout her school years. Her mother had worked in the same factory for years—a local factory that made seatbelt fabric.

During their children's school years, Fernanda got up at six each morning with her husband and got her children ready for school before she went to work. Today, she still follows that same routine when Theresa goes back to college and her other children leave for work.

Bad luck continued to haunt Theresa and her family. It was never ending. Shortly after her husband died, Fernanda was laid off from her job for several months and was forced to pay her costly health insurance. To make matters worse, a grease fire started in the kitchen of their home in Cumberland and spread to the second floor and roof.

The family had to seek temporary housing for several months while the house was being repaired, and Theresa commuted to Central Falls to finish her senior year.

In the meantime, Theresa, a solid A and B student and school leader (she was captain of the cheerleaders for four years, editor of the yearbook, member of the National Honor Society, student guide, etc.) was accepted at Roger Williams University in Bristol, Rhode Island, with financial assistance.

Fernanda and Theresa talked about how education came first in their family. Fernanda explained that when she was growing up in Portugal, working hard and doing well in school were family priorities and values that her father and mother held dearly.

Because of her need to work to support and care for her family, she regrets not having had the time to formally learn English or to continue her education in this country. A loving and caring woman, she is a devoted mother ("I love to have my family all together around me").

One of Theresa's middle school math teachers spoke about Theresa's devotion to her family. "When her father grew ill, Theresa grew up fast. She was always a good student, but now school became more important to her because she knew how important it was to her father as a way out of poverty. It was expected that she would go to college.

"She was always a dedicated student and would come after school to get extra help. She is worried about her mother having to work eleven hours a day and then taking care of her elderly mother-in-law on the weekends. Her goal is to graduate from college and get a good job so she can help her mother."

TEACHER PERCEPTIONS

In an e-mail to one of her friends during her first semester at college, Theresa indicated that she was adjusting to college life, but it was the first time she had not been in a culturally diverse school environment.

It was different being a minority. At Central Falls, her closest friends were a mixture of Dominicans, Colombians, Panamanians, and other nationalities.

At college she was making new friends and enjoying her classes, but was still fiercely loyal to her high school classmates and constantly kept in contact with them. She also returned home on weekends to work at KFC and be with her mother, whom she loves dearly.

After the first semester, Theresa called her favorite teachers to tell them that she had made the Dean's List. The teachers could hear the excitement in her voice. They totally understood how this special young lady managed to beat the odds and do so well in high school and now in college.

English teacher Deloris Grant offered some insight into what made Theresa so special. "Theresa is a social butterfly that should be running the White House social calendar for President Obama. She is the type of student who grows through social development and real-world connections.

"I put Theresa in charge of all major social events for my Advanced Placement class. I also put the Shakespeare competition I run each year in her hands. She organized the event with ease and placed second in the competition. I am convinced that Theresa used the acting methods and the memorization skills from this activity during the Advanced Placement testing and to gain entrance into college.

"She is a social being who works well in teams, and during class she took advantage of this opportunity for social emotional growth."

At first, Theresa wanted to be an English teacher, but she recently became aware that her strengths lie in public relations. Working in the corporate sector as a motivational speaker or a community organizer now appeals to her.

An example of her organizational and leadership skills occurred during the controversy concerning the high school teacher firing. Visibly upset with the pending action to fire all faculty members, she went into action, creating a Facebook page entitled "We Stand Together." She then contacted fifty people and told them to spread the word about what was happening and asked them to attend the school board meeting to speak out against the firings.

In two days, nine hundred people had responded. Two days after that, over four thousand responses had been logged. At the meeting, the first speaker was none other than Theresa Agonia, who gave an impassioned speech that drew a standing ovation when she finished. As she said later, "I just had to do something to help the teachers. They mean so much to me."

Theresa shared her feelings about Maeroff's comments. She totally disagreed with his thesis about her honors classes being watered down.

In fact, she attributed her first semester success at college to the rigor of her honors classes, especially the instruction by English honors teacher Deloris Grant, who made her work hard, challenged her to excel, and helped her raise her writing skills to a higher level.

She also mentioned social studies teacher Bob Scappini, who took time in each of his classes to prepare his students for the future demands of college. His inspirational college 101 talks about study skills, time management, and methods to meet the challenge of demanding college courses really resonated with Theresa.

Scappini, in turn, was very impressed with Theresa. He indicated that "Theresa was someone you want to say a silent prayer for to stop the suffering. I have never met anyone who has been through more adversity in a young life than she has.

"Even when she set her sights on attending Roger Williams, her acceptance letter was bittersweet. The college could not give her the needed scholarships. Theresa, being Theresa, started to make calls and write letters to resolve the problem. She was tenacious and found a solution."

Another one of her teachers summed it all up nicely when he said, "Theresa is simply someone special. She is the product of a strong family that came together after the loss of a beloved father and supported one another in any way they could.

"I spent a good deal of time with Theresa over her four years at the high school. I have rarely met someone who can work through so much adversity and still graduate near the top of her class and be a spokesperson and a role model for other students. Writing about her just doesn't do her justice.

"The best thing I can say is that I am not a touchy-feely person. I am by nature somewhat cynical. Very few people in my life have made me a better person. Theresa is one of them."

Theresa Agonia is indeed special. She is a young lady who has immense pride in and loyalty to her high school, is forever grateful to her teachers, has an appreciation for her Portuguese heritage, and clearly reflects what strong family values, hard work, determination, and perseverance can do in overcoming life's obstacles. Much can be learned from the example she has set for other Central Falls students.

CHAPTER 16

Bryant Estrada—An Independent Thinker

I was waiting to meet Bryant Estrada at the Shanghai Chinese restaurant (his choice) on Thayer Street, the busy commercial and fast food section in the heart of the Brown campus. It was our first meeting and the start of many conversations and e-mail exchanges we would have in the next few months.

Three Brown University male students were sitting at an adjacent table, in animated conversation, discussing a range of political issues. They were wearing old, torn dungarees and wrinkled flannel shirts that looked like they had been slept in the night before. Obviously, it is now fashionable to buy new clothes that look old and beat up at ridiculously high prices in places like the Urban Outfitters store directly across the street from the restaurant.

The Brown men tossed their slick leather jackets on a chair and ordered enough food to feed forty people. Facial hair, from muttonchops to three-day-old beards, complemented their unkempt mops of hair.

College is still the time of nonconformity, that time of initial independence, a time to study hard but also the only time you don't need to impress someone unless, of course, it's an attractive female or a professor you need to dazzle with your brilliance. The time to look and talk "corporate" was a way off. It could wait.

Bryant Estrada had attended Central Falls schools for twelve years. This young man had actually chosen to stay at Central Falls High School and had graduated number one in his class. How could a high school "dropout factory" adequately prepare someone like Bryant, the only son of immigrant Colombian parents, for success at an Ivy League school?

Shortly thereafter, Bryant arrived. He looked dramatically different from the three Brown men sitting nearby. He was neatly dressed, with closely cropped black hair and a welcoming smile. At five foot eleven and 230 pounds, he looked like a rugged linebacker from a preppy private school.

He said that he had been a hammer and discus thrower on the indoor track team in his junior year, and to his surprise he was elected team captain; however, he is not generally interested in sports and doesn't follow them closely. He has other interests.

Having been a frequent customer at the Shanghai Chinese restaurant, Bryant knew exactly what he wanted to order. He had a delightful sense of humor and a winning smile, which were evident when he said, "As you can see, I am not a slim guy. I love to eat. I am somewhat health conscious and have my cereal and fruit for breakfast. But I am a sucker for hamburgers. My only concession there is I look for meat market lean burgers rather than fast food type. It eases my conscience a bit."

After stuffing ourselves and consuming several pots of Chinese tea, I had learned a great deal about Bryant Estrada.

He told me that he went to a Catholic school pre-kindergarten program but received the remainder of his formal education in Central Falls schools. He credits his mother, father, and older sister and his participation in supplemental college preparation programs outside the school with his academic success.

Spanish is still the primary language at home, though his parents are fluent in English (although unlike Bryant they speak with a Spanish accent). He says his sister, who is two years older and is finishing her degree requirements at URI, speaks better Spanish than he does, but he counters, "I am a better writer than she is."

Bryant appeared to be a young man that sets goals, thinks critically, and knows what he wants and what is best for him. He chose to stay at Central Falls High School and didn't see the need to transfer after middle school to a private college preparatory school like Bishop Hendricken in Warwick.

He had a ready answer to why he made the decision to stay at his local high school. "Well, I reasoned that I had a better chance at finishing at the top of my class in Central Falls than at a private school.

A capable friend of mine decided to transfer to LaSalle Academy in Providence and did well, but I did better staying in Central Falls. I thought my chances of getting into an Ivy League college would be better. And this has been the case."

Bryant also explained that he and his family are managing the $51,000 tuition cost at Brown through several local, state, and Brown scholarships and federal grants but added, "My personal cost is one thousand dollars this year, but jumps to eight thousand next year."

As a young child, Bryant loved to read. He has always liked true-life novels, and in recent years he has read widely about adolescent problems and other types of victimization of young people, something that feeds his current interest in child psychology.

His parents want him to be a medical doctor, and at one time he shared that wish because he was an epileptic and had been introduced to the field of neurology at an early age. However, after working with inner-city kids and parents and taking a fascinating psychology course in his senior year, his career goals have shifted. He now wants to become a child psychologist.

In third grade, Bryant enrolled in the College Crusade, a program designed for low-income inner-city youth to gain scholarships for college by signing an agreement along with their parents to meet several character requirements and attend scheduled Crusader activities while in public school. The reward is a Crusade scholarship and ongoing mentoring while a Crusader.

Bryant successfully completed his Crusade contract and now works for the Crusade on Saturdays, when they run an enrichment program for students. In spite of his busy school schedule and working in a doctor's office on Sunday morning scanning and posting patient medical records online, he volunteers his time as a mentor for young inner-city children. He said that he really enjoyed helping young kids and their families and "gets along with them real well."

He also said that he was not totally dependent upon Central Falls High School for his learning. As one of his teachers remarked, "Bryant took advantage of every educational opportunity offered him outside the school walls." His enrollment in the Upward Bound Program at Rhode Island College for six semesters is a prime example and speaks to his thirst for learning, wherever that thirst can be satisfied.

Mariam Boyajian, longtime director of the Upward Bound program and a woman with a strong passion for her work, said, "Bryant went two full summers and took calculus courses, German, and college writing. We offer four courses each summer. These are rigorous, college-level courses on a higher level than those found in the high school curriculum.

"You should know that Bryant is one of fifteen grandchildren on his father's side. The Estradas are a very close family that highly values education, and several nieces and nephews have graduated from our program over the years. The Estrada clan has done quite well with us, and most have gone on to prestigious colleges.

"This is not a typical family connection. One of the Estradas' relatives, Elkin, is a 1987 graduate of our program. He is a successful Providence nephrologist and remains a strong supporter of our program. One of the high school teachers, Deloris Grant, and her sister, Viola Davis, recently nominated for an Academy Award for her best supporting actress role in 'Doubt,' are graduates of our program, as are other outstanding achievers on the state and national level.

"In a given year, we enroll 150 high school students, with twenty-five new spots each year reserved for Central Falls. We are essentially a successful forty-two-year-old supplemental educational program for low-income, first-generation college-bound students.

"We have a 99.9 percent high school graduation rate, a 98 percent college acceptance rate, and a 70 percent college retention/graduation rate. Bryant is simply following a family tradition to what we advertise will be a path to 'a more prosperous future.'"

Bryant spoke about the value of Upward Bound. He said, "It was a fantastic experience. The teachers were superb and set high standards. I also got to experience the college culture. After taking calculus at Rhode Island College, I found my high school calculus class to be nothing more than a refresher. I took calculus this past semester at Brown and did well. I owe Upward Bound a lot."

Before he finished his spring rolls, Brian responded to a question about his health. Bryant has had epilepsy all his life, and I asked whether it has affected his learning and social relationships.

"Not really. When I was a kid, my seizures were nocturnal and didn't occur at school. Because I now take medication and my seizures are under control, I consider myself a mild epileptic."

A math teacher who had Bryant in seventh and eighth grade talked about Bryant and his epilepsy. She has battled epilepsy all her life and helped Bryant cope with his illness.

She explains, "Bryant was always a hardworking student, but at first was very quiet in my classes. It took a few months before he approached me, but he finally told me about his epilepsy. I was always honest with my students about my seizures. At the time, he was embarrassed that he had this condition. We had several discussions, and I hope that I showed him that you can have a normal life even though you have epilepsy. I told him not to worry because his brain must have an abundance of electrical activity because he is so intelligent."

Bryant's last seizure was in December 2008, when he felt the pressure during college application and SAT time. He admitted that he didn't get much sleep during that period and thought that might have contributed to his seizure. Although he continues to play down his illness, one can't help but think that it must be a source of worry to him during high-stress periods of his life.

PARENTAL ASPIRATIONS

Fidel Estrada, Bryant's father, is a mechanical engineer at Andon Electronics Corporation, a tool-making company in Lincoln, Rhode Island. His mother, Rosalba, has worked for years at Tiffany and Company, a jewelry company in Cumberland, where she trains handicapped people, giving them the needed job skills for gainful employment.

Before leaving Colombia in the early '80s, Fidel received his associate's degree in mechanical engineering, and just missed receiving his bachelor's degree by a couple of credits before he left Colombia to join his father and other relatives in Central Falls. Rosalba also got her high school GED in this country while working full time and raising her two young children.

Both parents were highly engaged in Bryant's and his sister's educational journey through Central Falls schools. They were well known by teachers and school administrators because they were highly visible in the schools as volunteers, and they were recognized as interested parents who were highly invested in their children and their children's educational progress.

Fidel was president of the high school PTO, served on a task force I formed to improve school attendance, and led a one-man campaign to have high school teachers complete course syllabi. He was a tireless advocate of Central Falls schools as well as one of its most constructive critics.

He expected great things from Bryant. The two mottos he lives by best explain the high expectations he has for his children. The first is: "Failing is not an option. Do what you have to do to succeed." The second is: "It doesn't matter how good you are, you can be better." Mother and dad checked their children's homework daily, attended all school functions, and met with teachers frequently to check on the progress of their children.

One of his math teachers explains, "Bryant's father insisted that he take honors-level courses and be challenged academically. With his father, academics came first before any social activities.

"However, Bryant did manage to find a balance and still excel in the classroom. He was successful because his family taught him to be responsible and because he in turn also wanted what his parents wanted. He also was the type of student who would voluntarily stay after school if he didn't understand something in class until he 'got it.' That type of inner motivation is rare."

In some ways, Bryant was somewhat isolated from the rest of the student body. He was placed in accelerated honors classes from sixth grade to graduation. His peers were not involved in drinking, drug experimentation, or pressured into joining street gangs.

He said, "I knew that such stuff was going on, but the friends I hung with rejected such deviant behavior."

Students like Theresa Agonia, Guillermo Ronquillo, and Bryant were in the same classes together throughout high school and actually pushed one another to higher levels of achievement.

Bryant talked about what he did to relax and get a break from studying and his part-time jobs. He said Latin dancing was one of the things he likes to do to release tension. For several years he has performed in a community Latin dance group, and this year he joined the Latin dance company at Brown.

At a recent Brown performance, Bryant danced in two different numbers, not bad for a green freshman just beginning a new student activity. His friends say that when he dances, he thoroughly enjoys himself. Although he is a good-sized man among the slender bodies of the other performers, he is a smooth and polished dancer, swinging his female dance partners around the stage and holding them up high without strain at the end of the dance before respectfully bowing to the audience.

Bryant's other outlet is art. He credits his ceramic art teacher, Doris White, for discovering his love for visual art. Doris, a former graduate of Central Falls High School, explains, "When Bryant entered my Ceramics II class, I watched him grow and mature into a young man. He began to develop his technical and creative skill. Our relationship began to develop, and he began to express his educational goals through his works of art.

"In his senior year in my Advanced Ceramics class, he began to express his emotions, personality, and health issues in a somewhat abstract manner. At that time, I learned of his health problems and had several conversations with him about the matter. After that, his work began to explode with expression, technique, critical thinking, and problem-solving skills. The experience allowed him an opportunity to 'de-stress' and forget about life's pressures."

Doris was also impressed with Bryant's creativity. "I remember reading his college essay [appendix 2] and realizing that his expressive skills extended into his writing. I was amazed at his approach. He related his life to a board game, a creative, outside-the-box experience.

"I know Bryant will be successful because he is a hard worker, has clear goals, and parents who support him. I learned a great deal from Bryant. I would love to have a class full of Bryant Estradas."

Bryant admits he has missed art this year—that healthy outlet to free up his mind from intense study and let his creativity flow and his senses take over. Being a man of action and always thinking ahead, he found a way. He arranged to take an introductory course in visual art in his second semester and hopes to take other courses in this area in the future. Bryant mentioned several teachers who impressed him at the high school. He called Michael Occhi "an awesome teacher with a heart for students."

He also appreciated Bob Scappini's sound advice-giving in the last ten minutes of his history classes, when he talked about preparing for the SAT, putting an impressive college application together, and his constant reminder that college is not easy, so "you need to do now what it takes to prepare yourself."

He also appreciated Deloris Grant, his honors English teacher, and the fact that she challenged him and worked him hard. And of course, he would be forever grateful to his visual art and psychology teachers, who showed him beautiful new vistas he had never seen before.

Deloris Grant provided additional insight on what made Bryant such a special student.

"Bryant is the example of the student who uses auditory and visual learning to promote his own growth. I often use Bryant as an example to other students when I am giving reading instruction. Bryant often and consistently used sticky notes to mark reading questions and connections.

"If there was something he was confused by, he would see me after class or school to question me. Socrates would have loved Bryant because he was a student who used questioning to gain insight into complex concepts."

Like Theresa, Bryant offered his thoughts about Maeroff's mention of the lack of rigor in the high school curriculum, especially for advanced students.

His response again reflects his independent thinking and differs from the other students. "Sadly, I have to say yes, I do think the Central Falls education has been 'dumbed down.' It's really sad to admit it, but I personally believe it. However, I don't believe that Mr. Maeroff should make a general statement about all higher-achieving students.

"Despite his research in places he labels high school dropout factories, he doesn't really know what happens in those schools. I feel like I tried my best at the work I was given. I am not going to lie, there were times in high school where I didn't have any homework, or had teachers who were not serious about deadlines. It is nothing like that in college, any college.

"I do not think I was really prepared to go to an Ivy League institution, which I pretty much expected, but I have talked to many others who have gone to other less demanding and competitive schools and they feel the same way I do. I know I may be contradicting myself bringing up two opposing viewpoints, but I have mixed thoughts about the whole issue."

It should be noted at this point that Bryant had a solid first semester at Brown and is off to an excellent start in his second semester. But as his father says, "It doesn't matter how good you are, you can be better." Bryant therefore sets his own bar very high.

Bryant also offered his opinion about the expected firing of the entire high school faculty. He indicated that he didn't have all the facts and wondered what the real "behind the scenes" issues were.

On the surface, he thought firing all the teachers seemed like a disservice to those teachers who are already exceptional teachers and those teachers who have worked hard and made great strides over the years in improving their teaching and teaching results.

He felt an outside evaluation of teachers sounded like a good idea, but strongly disagreed with his father, who thought asking students to rate teachers was a good idea. He questioned student objectivity and pointed to their lack of maturity in order to rate teachers. He said to his dad, "I heard students saying they didn't like certain teachers because they were too demanding and had to work too hard in their classes."

Bryant admitted that there might be a handful of teachers who should be replaced, and if highly competent replacements could be found, it could help the school improvement initiative.

In his responses, Bryant was just being Bryant. He hesitates to say things unless he has a clear and thorough understanding of all the facts, can get answers to his questions, and can then reflect on and analyze all this information before stating his conclusions. Socrates would be proud of him.

CHAPTER 17

Guillermo Ronquillo—The Importance of Faith

It was time for the class salutatorian to give his address to his class-mates at the June 2009 Central Falls High School graduation. The auditorium was packed with proud parents, relatives, friends of the graduates, and teachers. They were in a joyous mood.

As he approached the podium, the audience quieted and watched Guillermo Ronquillo adjust the microphone and carefully place his speech notes on the podium shelf.

A young man of small stature with striking good looks, Guillermo spoke eloquently about his class and their achievements, until he got to the part of his speech where he talked about himself. His next series of comments would shock the audience.

"When I came into Central Falls High School, I was the kid that sat alone at lunch and had trouble finding a partner for science labs. Today, as I look out to you, I still don't see any friends." As Guillermo paused and saw the look of bewilderment on the faces in the audience, he smiled and said, "What I see is family."

Guillermo explained that he was fortunate in taking most of his classes with his fellow honors students and the caring and talented set of teachers who taught the honors courses. He also said he did not feel socially isolated, because he took most of his classes with same students in the honors curriculum. He explained, "Because the high school is such a small school, I also got to meet other people as well."

Guillermo spent his first school years in Santa Ana, El Salvador. His family came to neighboring Pawtucket to live with his uncle when he was in the fourth grade after his father, a physician, suffered a substantial financial loss in a failed business venture.

His father, Jesus, and mother, Patricia, who had a degree in psychology, did not speak English, and neither did Guillermo. Guillermo was placed in ESL classes in Pawtucket and learned English quickly. While in middle school, he was placed in Project Pass, a special accelerated program where he was able to take high school–level courses.

Guillermo's father had been an internist at a medical clinic in Santa Ana, and upon arriving in Pawtucket, he took the licensing exam to become certified as a physician in the United States. He worked part time and studied the rest of the time, but his lack of English fluency prevented him from gaining his license.

In order to support his family, he found work with ACP Cleaning Services, Inc., a Massachusetts-based company that cleans commercial buildings and is also involved in fire restoration, landscaping, painting, and other services. Currently, he is operations manager for the company.

Patricia, his mother, works as a child development specialist at the Kennedy Donovan Center in Fall River. She has an undergraduate degree in psychology and is presently completing her master's degree requirements in special education. Guillermo also has a fourteen-year-old brother, Diego, who is a middle school student.

As professional parents, the Ronquillos placed a high value on education. His dad taught Guillermo basic math while he was learning Spanish in Bible classes at the Seventh Day Adventist Church in Santa Ana. Because of his exposure to the medical profession at an early age, he has always wanted to be a medical doctor.

The Ronquillos left Pawtucket in 2006 and bought a home in Central Falls. Guillermo entered the ninth grade as a newly registered student and surprisingly was assigned to regular education classes.

Naturally shy and not the type who wanted to attract attention, he was befriended by some male students whom he described as "being into some bad things." Wanting to fit in and looking for acceptance, he began wearing offbeat shirts that were three times too big for him, and baggy pants that hung loosely on his hips. Seeing this transformation, his parents became quite concerned and wondered what had happened to him.

Guillermo felt terribly miscast in his new high school setting. For over a month, he found himself in classes that were not challenging him—coursework that covered content he had already taken in his accelerated Pawtucket middle school program. He started to lose motivation and interest in his studies. He also knew he was associating with questionable friends—the type that would get him into big trouble.

Although he was going downhill, he never told his parents. He said he prayed to God for a long time to have his current situation changed. After a month, he took matters into his own hands and finally convinced a guidance counselor to schedule him into honors classes, where he knew he belonged. It was in the honors classes where he found "his family" and where he was challenged to excel academically.

Throughout his life, Guillermo felt a sense of duty to his God and to his parents, because they have "always protected and supported me." He is an active member of the Seventh Day Adventist Church in Providence, where he is very involved with the youth group, preaches, and plays on the church soccer team.

In his college essay (appendix 1), he explains how his faith has given him an inner confidence and a special competitiveness. He says, "In my life, it is not a battle or a struggle for survival in nature which brings out the best in me, but rather a struggle for success. Furthermore, it is this competitive nature that allows me to fight and overcome all that stands in my way."

In his essay, he mentions an incident that ignited his competitive nature. "In my first year of ESL class, my teacher was trying to explain to me how in English as opposed to the Spanish language, an adjective can come before a noun. When she saw I was having a hard time, she got up to leave and said, 'stupid kid' under her breath. Though I did not speak English fluently, I knew exactly what she had said.

"This single incident awoke my competitive nature and made me work harder. One year later, I was moved into mainstream English classes."

Another incident was even more dramatic because it was Guillermo's first exposure to blatant racial discrimination. At the age of fourteen, he was with his mother and aunt in a New Bedford mall getting fitted for a tuxedo. While waiting for Guillermo to be fitted, his mother and aunt were sitting down, chatting in Spanish. All of a sudden, an old man sitting next to them shouted, "Stop talking in Spanish and go back to where you came from!"

The Ronquillos were shocked and offended. Rather than stop with his insults, the old man began shouting at the top of his voice, "United we stand, divided we fall!" He kept repeating this chant as Guillermo watched his mother and aunt cry. The man's wife was totally embarrassed and hurriedly got her ranting husband to leave.

The mall incident further contributed to Guillermo's competitive fire. He is determined to overcome all obstacles, including racial discrimination, and not let them get in the way of his future success. Who knows, in a few years the old man may be sitting in a waiting room waiting to see an internist. Perhaps he will recognize Guillermo when he shakes his hand and enters his office.

In response to Maeroff's contention about honors classes in high schools like Central Falls being of questionable quality, Guillermo disagreed, but does admit that many non-honors classes are at a low level.

He said, "They were classes where hardly any homework was assigned and the material being taught was clearly not at the high school level. Moreover, students seemed to show little interest in learning, which in turn causes teachers to have low expectations. Now, I am not saying all non-honors classes are at a low level, it depends on the teacher."

He cautioned that any outside evaluation of teachers has to take into consideration that during his four years, the high school was in a constant state of flux with a new principal and schedule each year, changing graduation portfolio requirements, a separation of freshman and sophomores from juniors and seniors, sudden cancellation of important courses like physics (although an after-school course was finally arranged), and the recent closing of one of the new academies.

He also feels that Central Falls can't afford to have programs like SAT preparation classes and teacher tutoring programs that other schools have, and this lack contributes to low student test scores.

He mentioned his history teacher, Bob Scappini, and life science teacher, Joshua LaPlante, as examples of high-quality teachers. He is upset that teachers like those two have to go through the process of being terminated and then reapply for their jobs. He questions why thorough and effective teacher evaluations were not done prior to the receipt of their termination notices.

He liked Scappini's creativity and the way he varied his teaching. For example, after introducing a particular topic, he asked his students to pull content related artifacts out of his "interactive box."

Red tags were attached to the artifacts indicating a class project they had to complete. Scappini required the students to use dynamic and synthesis reading techniques in their research and then present a summary of their findings to the class. At other times, he would start his class with a provocative statement, like "At times it's all right to cheat," as a way to spark debate and get his students to think and present their positions with coherence, logic, and clarity.

Guillermo really feels indebted to Joshua LaPlante and credits him for cultivating his love for the life sciences, especially after LaPlante, who teaches both honors and regular courses, involved him in an anatomy and physiology partnership he arranged at a local hospital.

He said that LaPlante "constantly found new ways to teach, was hard but fair, and consistently motivated students to do more. In turn, a student would come out of his class with broad knowledge and great enthusiasm for learning."

TEACHER PERCEPTIONS

Teachers also had nice things to say about Guillermo and spoke about how he was a special student and a special young man.

Although LaPlante admits that some students in his honors classes didn't fit the "honors" category, he considers Guillermo a student who would have outperformed his top students at a very competitive private school where he had taught previously.

He mentioned how Guillermo is at Providence College on full scholarship in their honors program, where he made the Dean's List in his first semester, just missing a perfect 4.0 grade point average.

LaPlante further elaborates on what makes Guillermo an extraordinary student: "Guillermo continuously demonstrates integrity, honesty, and a strong work ethic. He is responsible, nonconfrontational, disciplined, and goal oriented. He has purpose, and above all else, he has the potential to become a successful member of the local and global community. He exemplifies leadership, commitment, compassion, and moral integrity.

"He is an inspiration to me, and it is because of students like Guillermo that I have chosen and remain in education. When all else seems to be discouraging, there are people like him who bring back that emotional connection that brought us into teaching. Guillermo was the type of student that challenged me to be better, and at times he was my 'go to person' for self-evaluation."

Deloris Grant saw another side of Guillermo in her English classes. "Guillermo is a brilliant, creative writer who improved his ability to write with each lesson and strategy that was given to him. His unique style of oration was masterful. It was amazing when I first gave him the role of Shylock in the *Merchant of Venice* in the local Shakespearean competition.

"His initial cold reading was stilted and his volume was too low. He did not understand the nature of the character. After giving him constructive feedback and, time on stage to perform, he improved with each rehearsal, until he achieved perfection to the point where he won awards in the local and state levels.

"He is the type of student who uses feedback to achieve exemplary writing and oral communication development, and he exemplifies the type of student that grows with proper instruction that targets his area of needs."

Yes, Guillermo is a student teachers will remember. As Joshua LaPlante implied, he is a young man that restores faith in you as a teacher and in the power and influence of good teaching.

Mr. Maeroff would have to admit that Guillermo got as much out of the Central Falls honors program as he would have from high-powered honors programs offered in affluent suburban high schools across the country, if not more.

In Central Falls, Guillermo was fortunate to have competition from a handful of gifted students like Bryant Estrada and Theresa Agonia. The three students became good friends and thrived on the friendly competition among themselves, especially the academic class rank contest between Bryant and Guillermo. Both young men share part-time jobs in the same doctor's office and have great mutual respect for one another.

All three students have different personalities and different abilities, but as Guillermo said to a waiting and anxious graduation audience, "we are family," and that was the glue that helped all of them achieve academic success.

CHAPTER 18

George Carle—A Basketball Dream

The odds that George Carle would graduate from high school and gain acceptance into college had to be at least 500 to 1. The odds that he will eventually receive his college diploma may be greater than that. But don't bet against him or his mother, either.

Unlike Theresa, Bryant, and Guillermo, George was not an honors student. He is, however, more representative of the majority of students that come from low-income Central Falls families who struggle economically and face myriad problems outside the school, problems that interfere with the ability of their children to do well in school.

As a young child, George didn't like to read, and he still finds it a task he doesn't enjoy. He also never had two parents who made education a high priority in his young life. He is one of thirteen children his birth father had, and his birth father is a man he seldom sees and who never lived with his mother or the three children she had with him.

While a young boy, George moved with his mother nine times, from Providence to Central Falls to Woonsocket to Philadelphia to Buffalo to Cape Verde to Central Falls to Pawtucket and finally in 2005 back to Central Falls, where George entered the eighth grade.

To understand the challenges George has faced in his lifetime, you need to know the background of his mother, Rosa Rosado, and her intense love and undying commitment to George and his two younger brothers, sixteen-year-old Joshua and fourteen-year-old Christian, currently students at Central Falls High School. Her life story reads like fiction.

Now in her mid-thirties, Rosa has suffered from being bipolar and was on medication for years. She has had a sad and conflict-ridden past. She admits that she made poor choices in her twenties and early thirties and takes full responsibility for her sometimes uncontrollable physical aggression, rage, and loss of emotional control that hurt other people.

She also regrets having lived a reckless and selfish life that included buying and selling drugs. However, throughout all her troubles, she passionately protected and cared for her children, something she would have done even if, as she says, it had required "selling myself on the street corner, although thankfully it never came to that."

In 2006, after a wake-up call involving a police incident with her sons, Rosa turned her life around and today is a successful streetworker at the Institute for the Practice and Study of Nonviolence, working primarily in Central Falls with students and families who are victims of violent crimes.

Rosa is an outgoing person who readily shares her life mistakes in order to demonstrate how far she has come, and to give hope to troubled youth that they too can overcome their past indiscretions and lead purposeful lives.

A dynamic, attractive, and talkative lady with a big heart and ready smile, she relates well with young people, especially teenagers. It's hard to believe that this woman had such a tumultuous past.

Rosa grew up in a tough section of Providence, and at sixteen she dropped out of Hope High School. She explained that she grew up enduring various types of abuse and violence, such as rape and assaults, but also admitted that eventually she too "became part of the problem" by committing violent acts on others in order to retaliate against people who upset her. "It took me a long time to realize that my causing physical and emotional harm to others was not right. I lost my emotional control, especially when I got angry."

A member of a large Puerto Rican family, her oldest brother died from a gunshot wound and her second brother suffered an injury related to a drunk-driving accident that has confined him to a wheelchair for life without the ability to walk, talk, or eat unless assisted by a nurse.

She speaks of her early life, when she was physically assaulted by a jealous boyfriend. "I was pregnant as a teenager with my first child when my boyfriend ran up behind me and struck me with a beer bottle, leaving a large laceration on my face and the side of my head. As a result, I spent ten hours in the trauma unit at Rhode Island Hospital."

A tall, physically impressive looking woman who is affectionally called "Moaks" by her friends and family, she readily admits that she committed quite a few violent acts against others, particularly after marrying her husband in 1995, when she adopted his lifestyle and became a member of his gang—a gang that was heavily into selling drugs.

She admits, "I became accustomed to easy money and easy streets. The streets in Central Falls were full of people who made it easy for me to do the bad things I did."

In the next few years, she was arrested three times and sent to prison, once for a narcotics violation and twice for physical assault. While in prison for short periods and separated from her children, she admitted she felt empty, missing her boys terribly, and vowed to turn her life around.

She said, "I had to get out of my present situation fast." So she and her young family left Central Falls and tried to start over in other places.

She got a few good jobs in the Buffalo area but again made some bad choices, especially when she followed her deported boyfriend to Cape Verde. Shortly thereafter, she returned to Central Falls.

Her struggles in Central Falls however continued. "I tried to find a job and a place for me and my kids. We were in homeless shelters on four different occasions. Unfortunately, to support my family, I was still selling drugs and getting high and found myself on the mercy of the courts. It was at this time that my kids' father took me twice to court, trying to get out of paying child support. He failed, and thank God I continued to have full custody of my children."

It wasn't until 2006 that an event occurred that changed her life. Her apartment was raided by the police, and they charged her with possession of drugs. As she entered her apartment, she saw a policeman with a gun placed at her thirteen-year-old son's head.

After she was released on bail the next day, she ran into the confidential informant who had helped in the raid, and, as she put it, "I assaulted her to the extreme."

Three months later she was picked up on the warrant for the assault, placed on probation, and ordered to undergo drug counseling, which she successfully completed. From that point on, Rosa Rosado was a changed woman.

It had taken a gun to her young son's head to bring her to her senses, and she could see that her boys were now being directly affected and were starting to go in an unhealthy direction in school and with their choice of friends. She knew that she was at a critical juncture in her life. She had to turn her life around and never look back.

The legal system had given her a last chance to get her life together. After a period of unemployment, and with Principal Legault's assistance, she got a job as streetworker with the Institute for the Study and Practice of Nonviolence.

It was a perfect fit. She embraced the opportunity to help other kids and families through tragic and violent experiences that she knew all too well. She was credible, persuasive, and convincing. Teaching nonviolence became her new passion, and her life of drugs was now finally behind her.

Throughout all the turmoil, heartache, and pain, Rosa remained dedicated and loyal to her three boys. She never abandoned them, because they were always the centerpiece of her life, the one area where she had to be responsible. She was fiercely dedicated to her sons and feverishly protected them because she knew the dangers that lurked in the dark city streets.

She didn't want them to make the same mistakes she had made and associate with the wrong crowd like she had. She wanted them to have dreams of a better life, and she always knew that educational success and attainment were the keys to realizing those dreams. This belief had been reinforced every time she sought employment and found that her lack of education was a major handicap in getting a well-paying job.

Her constant motto to her boys became, "If you can dream it, you can do it." Making education a priority in their lives became a major goal in her life.

GEORGE'S DREAM

George Carle was sitting at a small table in the kitchen of a small apartment on the second floor of a three-story tenement building directly across from Central Falls High School.

George, Rosa, his two brothers, and Rosa's boyfriend, David, who is affectionately referred to as uncle and "White Heat" by the boys, currently live in the apartment, although George spends the week living on campus at URI, where he currently is enrolled.

Rosa has lived with David for the last few years and calls him "one of the best things that has happened to me and the boys in a long time." Rosa says her boys respect David and that he has brought needed stability and support to the household.

George talked about his dream of playing college basketball and getting his college degree in the process. "My goal is to play Division I basketball and down the road become a professional basketball player. I tried to walk on at URI, but didn't make it.

"My plan now is to transfer to a Division II school next year, do well and get some attention, and maybe get a shot to play in Europe after I graduate. I have been working out and my coach has told me that a couple of Division II schools are interested in me. I plan on following up on those possibilities. We'll see what happens."

Becoming a pro basketball player is a dream that many successful high school basketball players have but seldom achieve. George knew there would be bumps in the road, but he believed in himself and his talent and was now more realistically considering the options available to him. He knew getting his college degree was more important to his future, but why not use his basketball talent as a ticket to that degree? He loved the game of basketball.

When asked about his first semester at URI, he said it didn't go well. He had failed two of the five courses he had taken and was now in a program where he could repeat those courses and take others in an attempt to remain in school for the fall semester. He has been told that he needs to get his grade point average up in order to transfer to a Division II college, and is off to a good start in his second semester at URI.

George explained his academic struggles both in high school and now in college. "In high school, I was a late bloomer and only got real serious about my studies after my junior year. My poor literacy skills held me back. I finished with about a C average.

"My high school teachers helped me a lot, especially with extra tutoring and by giving me strong recommendations that resulted in my being accepted at URI in their Talent Development Program. Although

I might not have been prepared for college in my first semester, I know I can improve my academics and get my college degree. I will never give up."

George is six foot three and 185 pounds. He is a courteous, soft-spoken, self-effacing young man and is delightfully laid back. He gave thoughtful responses and praised his mother, whom he called his biggest cheerleader and confidante. He was a young man you liked immediately.

Principal Liz Legault and George's basketball coach and science teacher, Joshua LaPlante, provided insightful feedback on George Carle, the basketball player, and on George Carle, the young man and student.

As a veteran principal in the school district, Legault has known Rosa and her boys for several years. She agreed that George was a fast "academic closer" and a very talented and celebrated basketball player.

"He's a smart kid, but developmentally delayed. He's a quiet, humble young man and not an attention-getter given his celebrity status. In fact, his mother many times puts him in the limelight that he really doesn't want."

Liz mentioned how Rosa is such a purpose-driven woman and how much she has matured in the role of streetworker. She reports that she is very conscientious about keeping her temper in check.

"She is a deceptively bright lady with street smarts. Her boys are her life, and believe me she keeps them on a very tight rope. She also has told me she doesn't want any teenage fathers in her family. After a rough start a few years ago, we now get along fine. I think she is a remarkable lady."

George mentions that his mother is strict, but he realizes she has to be. He said she might be a bit overprotective, something that Rosa disagrees with when she explains, "There is no such thing as being overprotective, especially in Central Falls, where there have been two teenagers who recently have died in shootings.

"My boys have strict curfews. If the older boys go out at 7:00 p.m. they must be back by 9 p.m. I want to know where they are going, what they are doing, and who they are doing it with."

When asked if George's dream of playing Division I basketball was realistic, another of George's basketball coaches, Brian Crookes, said,

"George was a strong, tenacious player who played underneath the basket in our small high school division. In college, he would need to be a two guard and have a better perimeter shot, something he needs to work on. However, at this stage, he definitely would excel at a Division II school."

Crookes continued, "I am impressed with George as a basketball player, but I am even more impressed with him as a person. He was selected as captain of our team in his senior year and cared more about the team than his own exploits. He is a humble, unselfish young man with an incredible work ethic.

"In fact, in my years of coaching I never had anyone who worked harder than George. His improvement from his freshman year to his senior year was remarkable. He has unlimited potential and because of his determination will just get better.

"He earned all-division honors in our small school league, but impressed in regional all-star games with players from larger schools. If George continues to improve and work as hard as he does, I wouldn't rule out his chances at this point of playing professional basketball somewhere after college just yet."

George was asked about his social relationships. He said it is easy for him to make friends. When asked how he is perceived by his friends he said, "They see me as a clown and goofball."

When asked if he saw himself as a role model for younger kids like his brothers, he reluctantly responded, "Well, maybe. Yeah, I guess so."

When told that his mother thinks he is a sweet kid and calls him by his nickname, "Little Porgy," he gets embarrassed.

You can sense the admiration and gratitude he has for his mother and the strong bond between them. He understands and accepts what she has been through and appreciates how she has been fully and completely dedicated to him and his brothers in spite of her troubled past.

He doesn't want to disappoint her or himself as he chases his dreams. Although they have entirely different personalities, George has adopted his mother's determined spirit. He says he will never give up his quest for a college degree.

Joshua LaPlante beautifully summarizes who George Carle is and what makes him special. LaPlante was one of three teachers George credits with motivating him and pushing him to work harder and improve academically. The others were the late Michael Occhi and his French teacher, Hope Evanoff.

LaPlante feels that George Carle is very impressive. "George's past focus was not so much on academics but more on athletics. He was the most confident person on the court but lacked the same level of confidence in the classroom. It almost seemed as though there was a bit of fear to be a standout in class.

"He did what he needed to in school to be successful but made measurable changes during his senior year. I had George in my Anatomy and Physiology class, and as time moved on he began to see things in a way that made him recognize his academic potential.

"He is a bright young man who matured significantly in the one year that I got to know him. He really began to challenge himself to think past the obvious, and learned to explore his thoughts, building confidence and academic self-esteem.

"George has a clear sense of identity and has great potential to be a great leader. He is well respected by the faculty, students, and community members of Central Falls and in surrounding communities. He has a clear vision to be different.

"I am aware of the hardships that he and his family have endured and find it incredible for someone to recognize that they have the ability to do more, and actually do more, especially when the odds are against them. I really credit his mother, who, through her own personal growth that was inspired by her children, has made amazing efforts to show support and provide motivation for her children to succeed.

"George is another student that should be modeled in Central Falls because of his perseverance and genuine kindness and respect for others." LaPlante has perfectly captured George Carle and his mother, Rosa Rosado. Their indomitable will is obvious. I wouldn't bet against them.

CHAPTER 19

Summary

The four students profiled in this book were school achievers. Three of the students were honors students and represented the top layer of their class. The fourth student, George Carle, was a class leader and a struggling average student.

It is fair to say that profiling just the achievers shows only the best side of the student body. What about the bulk of students in the school who are failing?

For example, what about that failing student who has no intention of doing any better? What about profiling several dropouts? And then there is the average student who could do better, but doesn't, or the average student who actually is an overachiever. Why showcase only the "jewels" in the school?

If you surveyed urban teachers, they would tell you that teaching the unmotivated, low-achieving student with a poor self-image is a far greater challenge than teaching students in the honors program. Without question, profiling different types of student learners in inner-city high schools would be very instructive and more representative of an urban high school student body. It would also make an interesting second book or series of provocative newspaper articles.

But there is a reason for selecting the four students showcased in this book. This was meant to be a positive book, presenting successful urban students in order to analyze the keys to their success and share those findings with all Central Falls parents.

Admittedly, not all students can be valedictorians or salutatorians. Nor can all students be popular class leaders. However, all students can learn and be made to feel they are worthwhile individuals. Hopefully, present and future Central Falls students will learn from the examples of hard work, determination, and perseverance set by Theresa, Bryant, Guillermo, and George that educational achievement is essential for a successful future. Like the four students illustrated in this book, all Central Falls students need to get serious about doing well in school.

The hope is that from the four success stories, Central Falls parents will also gain some valuable insight into their own situations and appreciate the critical importance of assisting their children in realizing educational success, completing high school, and continuing on to post-secondary education. This is especially true in the twenty-first century Information Age and with the emerging New Economy.

Much can therefore be learned from reading the case studies in this book. For example, one thing was very clear: The four students all had determined parents who encouraged their children to work hard in order to succeed in school. Their parents had high expectations for them, closely followed their progress in school, and got to know their teachers. A quality education for their children was not just a priority, it was a top priority in their lives, in spite of their socioeconomic status.

Rosa Rosado knows many parents and feels that too many of them want their children to succeed in school but don't make the personal commitment they should, and they end up making excuses for their children. She feels that using poverty as an excuse is a weak reason, and she should know. Pointing to teachers as the main problem for low student achievement is not fair; in her opinion, it's the parents.

Much is made over the fact that Central Falls High School has been a "low-achieving school" for seven years. What is not known is that until a new, tough attendance policy was approved four years ago, only about sixty-five percent of the student body was in school on any given day.

Attendance, of course, was always high in the honors classes, but it took over two years to increase the overall attendance rate to slightly over ninety percent for the full student body. The problem was finally rectified after appealing to and educating parents, and by making the school a welcoming and more relevant place where students want to be—a place where success, not failure, awaits students.

Considering the residential instability problem, with students constantly moving in and out of the school district adding to poor student attendance and the tardiness problems, it is difficult to hold teachers fully accountable for low student achievement.

Imagine teaching a class where one-third of your class is missing each day. No teacher can improve student achievement if the students aren't in school. Yes, it may have taken too long for the attendance and tardiness problems to be resolved, but as poverty has risen in this poorest community in the state, the challenge to increase student achievement has become more difficult. Parents, however, still have to be held accountable and see that their children go to school each day.

TWO RESPECTED TEACHERS SPEAK OUT

The book also traces the challenges to reforming urban schools, and the role teachers and poverty play in the difficult task of turning around a failing school.

Joshua LaPlante, a masterful teacher who teaches a wide range of students, summarizes the challenges best. "Once you evaluate the uncontrollable variables that exist for the vast majority of our students, it becomes a question of how can those students survive and be successful.

"Of course, it is essential to maintain high academic standards, but in urban schools the difficulty is magnified significantly, because not only do students need to meet the standards of their teachers, the state, and the school community, but they have to do it while learning English, raising families, working, being sure to have a place to sleep and food to eat, and essentially surviving each day without being consumed by all the negative influences that exist in urban communities."

Deloris Grant is a superb teacher and shared some final thoughts on parents, personal motivation, and the need for quality teaching.

Like Joshua LaPlante, she wouldn't ever call herself a master teacher, but nevertheless she is one. Not only are the two teachers dedicated, creative, and bright, but they also share one important thing—they view themselves as works in progress, always learning and growing, trying to find new ways to motivate and reach urban students while at the same time pushing them to succeed.

They are demanding teachers who have high standards and prod their students constantly, but they find a way to provide that extra special assistance so their students can succeed, not fail. Whatever it takes, they walk that extra mile.

It was interesting to get Deloris's reaction to Maeroff's comments about advanced classes in urban high schools.

"I take offense when I am told that I teach the minimum just because I am an educator at an urban school. I emphasize higher-order thinking skills. I introduce my students to many college-level texts and practice high-level, demanding writing and speaking, and that is why Theresa, Bryant, and Guillermo were prepared for college work. I will not take all the honors. They came with willing hearts and minds to learn, as well as a respect for learning."

This leads us to the question of inner motivation. Why do some students succeed while others who might be equally capable fail?

Deloris sheds light on that question. She grew up and graduated from Central Falls High School. She said her family was dirt poor, and at one time was the only black family in the city. Her mother had an eighth grade education, and her father had a sixth grade education. Although her family was poor, they made sure she and her four sisters attended school each day. No excuses. Additional support for her at home was through books.

However, she didn't get serious about going to college until two of her high school teachers encouraged her to take advanced courses and told her that going to a good college was well within her reach. It was a case of not believing in yourself until someone else believes in you.

Her teachers made all the difference. Deloris is now a proud Central Falls High School teacher who is returning the favor and making a real difference in the lives of her high school students.

One theory about self-motivation is that it is inherent, something you are either born with or not born with. It refers to people who have an "inner fist," a special drive to achieve.

Guillermo talks of such motivation in his graduation speech. These are people who are ambitious, welcome challenges, and reach high. They are not afraid to test themselves. Like olympic athletes, they set goals and are committed to working hard to achieve those goals. They don't let failure or other obstacles stop them in their quest.

It is difficult to believe that personal motivation is not more of a reflection of where you were born and raised, the friends you have, and, most importantly, who your parents happen to be. Family values, expectations, and the role models in your life are constantly contributing to the shaping and development of a young person's self-esteem, personal confidence, and future ambitions.

However, some young people who lack the support systems mentioned above overcome these handicaps and lead successful and productive lives. Despite their background, something inside them motivates them and compels them to beat the odds. It may be that "inner fist"—something you can't explain or deny. But these young people are the exception, not the rule.

The best road to future success is to have parents and role models who love and believe in you. They demonstrate this by setting high expectations and helping you realize that achieving your dreams means working hard, doing well in school, and, in the words of Fidel Estrada, "doing whatever it takes."

Joshua LaPlante mentioned that it takes wise and committed parents and teachers to instill the will to learn, the work ethic, and a sense of hope in underprivileged inner-city students.

Deloris also offered her opinion on why some students are highly motivated to achieve while others are not, and the influence teachers have in raising student expectations.

"Many of the high-achieving students I serve have this desire to have a close relationship with one or two teachers. These students also participate in some form of activity and have one or two close friends who are also involved in the school culture or in the community. For instance, if we look at students who are not successful, the one common thread these students have is lack of ambition to participate in the school culture, and they are most likely to have attendance issues.

"Unfortunately, these students do not have parents at home who support their academic needs. It is difficult to determine where the successful student gets his ambition, but I feel it is grounded in adversity and community support. What happens when the student leaves the building? Where do they go?

"This is what also determines success. I often wonder why certain students have this need to achieve while others have fated themselves to a less ambitious road. I try to instill in every student that they are capable of anything they try hard enough to achieve. I also believe that if a child is born in poverty, it is important to let them know that they can still rise above their situation."

A FINAL WORD

It is my hope that Central Falls parents will profit from reading the success stories of the four students presented in this book and realize that they have a critical responsibility to make the education of their children a top priority in their lives. Although it may be difficult, they must find the time and the will to support their children and take advantage of the educational opportunities that are available to them and their children in the schools and in the greater community.

Parents need to attend school functions and get to know their children's teachers. They need to educate themselves and learn to ask the right questions about their children's school progress or lack thereof, and help their children succeed in school any way they can.

They need to be vigilant parents and good role models, and they must teach their children responsibility. The list goes on and on. The educators call it "parent engagement," but it is more all-encompassing than that. It is a change of attitude and the willingness to make a personal and continuing commitment to the education of your child.

Meanwhile, the battle on how best to improve Central Falls High School drags on. On February 22, 2010, the Central Falls School Board of Trustees, at a raucous meeting filled with AFT sympathizers, approved the firing of all members of the high school staff, informing the commissioner of education that they will be adopting the "turnaround model" due to failure to reach agreement with the teachers' union on the superintendent's transformational model plan.

In the crowded auditorium, the terminated teachers stood when their names were called during the reading of the motion, several breaking out in tears, others standing proudly, others looking defiant. It was a sad moment.

Because there is only one small high school in the community and no other school where terminated teachers can be transferred or assimilated, teachers will be out of a job at the end of June. In a district financed entirely by state funds and federal grants, the action is unprecedented.

The story has received nationwide coverage in major news stations around the country, including CBS, NBC, FOX, and CNN. Talk radio stations and Internet websites feed the media frenzy. President Obama, U.S. Secretary of Education Duncan, Governor Carcieri, and the *Providence Journal* all issued public statements in support of Superintendent Gallo and the board's position.

The national AFT president issued a statement in support of the local teachers' union, and the Rhode Island executive council of the AFL-CIO has filed unfair labor practices with the state. The conflict has become the center of national attention and a national debate on the best approach to turn around chronically low-performing inner-city high schools.

The lines are still drawn, with divisiveness spreading throughout the community. The students are upset and teachers are angry. Many of the teachers are deflated, especially the exceptional ones, who feel they have had their character and reputation damaged and their professional status compromised.

There are four months left in the school year, and many people are wondering how much teaching and learning will be affected by a controversy that looks like it won't go away soon. The school is in turmoil, and teacher bitterness is very apparent. One teacher hung an Obama doll in effigy in his classroom, an action that was condemned by both the union president and the superintendent of schools.

The AFT leadership eventually employed a new strategy. They publicly stated that they were open to accepting some of the transformation model preconditions set by Dr. Gallo if she would sit down and negotiate the details with them.

Gallo indicated she would be willing to accept their offer if both sides could agree on changes needed to improve the school. If an agreement is reached, she would consider rescinding the termination notices sent to teachers.

Three days after the public announcements, the AFT descended upon the board of regents at its regular board meeting held in the West Warwick High School auditorium. At a rally outside the school, Jane Sessums, president of the Centrals Falls Teachers' Union, waved a handful of petitions at the crowd, claiming she had over ten thousand signatures on them supporting her union's position.

Later, over five hundred teacher supporters from across the state and beyond filled the audience seats, many wearing red, the Central Falls High School color. Commissioner Gist and the regents were experiencing a Rhode Island teacher union rally up close for the first time.

Several union supporters came to the microphone trying to convince the commissioner and regents that they were for high school reform, but felt it should be a collaborative process, insisting that wasn't the way it was being done. They claimed that "as professionals," they were ready to sit down and resolve the current impasse.

Superintendent Gallo sat quietly in the front row of the auditorium. She later stated to the press that she was disappointed the union hadn't decided to call off their rally, but instead decided to display its political power and might. Although harassed and vilified during the past several weeks, she has courageously stood her ground while maintaining the steadfast support of the Central Falls School District's Board of Trustees.

Gallo has paid a heavy personal price for the action she has taken. She has received hate mail and been booed at public meetings. One e-mail was particularly upsetting and outright cruel. She told a newspaper it read as follows, "The writer said he wishes the most terminal cancer on my family and children and their children, and that I live long enough to see them suffer." The hateful words made her cry.

Others want Gallo to just go away or retire. Her public response to that was, "Quitting is not in my vocabulary. Retiring is not in my plan until Central Falls is successful."

But like the board chair, Anna Cano Morales, Fran Gallo is disturbed by the persisting failure and struggle of Central Falls students—a struggle Anna has described as having "moved our conscience and our soul." Both ladies will not quit.

It is early March 2010. Will this dispute end amicably with a resolution jointly reached by both parties? Will the last resort, the reconstitution of the school, occur? This is not a predictable situation, and only time will tell.

However, if reconstitution is the course taken, it will be interesting to see if this approach will actually work in Central Falls High School. There are so many variables that come into play that it is difficult to speculate on outcomes.

It is best to close this book with this simple parable from an anonymous source:

There was a farmer who for years felt his harvest was not plentiful enough; it never seemed to get better. He tried all types of new fertilizers and seed. But still, his crop failed. He became very disappointed.

As a last resort, he burned all his fields and brought in new rich loam and expensive seed. His hope was for a better yield. He didn't know what would happen.

The farmer had no guarantee that the new seeds would germinate in the new soil and yield a better harvest. It had partially worked in some neighboring farms, but failed in others. Would it work on his farm?

The farmer feared going from the known to the unknown. But he felt he had no choice, because the known was unacceptable. The yield never seemed to get better as each year passed. What did he have to lose in starting anew?

A Final Note: In May 2010, after four months of bloody warfare and 40 hours of mediation, the Central Falls School District and the Central Falls Teachers' Union reached an agreement that averted the mass firing of the high school staff and saved the jobs of 93 staff members. This settlement followed Superintendent Gallo's receipt of more than 700 teacher applications throughout the country from those wanting to teach in the embattled high school.

The teachers' union agreed to increase the school day by 25 minutes and provide one hour of scheduled tutoring before school or after school each week. Common teacher planning time was eliminated during the school day with the recouped time to be used for additional instruction. Planning time would now be scheduled after school. Teachers would receive a $3,000 stipend from a new federal grant for time spent after school helping students.

Other union concessions provided the school administration with new authority. They would now have sole discretion to make teacher assignments and identify an evaluation system for 2010–2011 that could include third-party evaluators and serve as the basis for teacher rehiring in 2011. In the areas of promotions, transfers, and new hires, seniority would no longer define job placement. The union may file grievances about the process of placement decisions, but not the decisions themselves.

In essence, the provisions needed to implement the transformational model for school improvement was now in place and the ugly battle had finally come to an end.

Meanwhile, the farmer finds himself with what he hopes will be new fertile ground to plant his old seeds. Will this strategy work? Will he finally realize an increased yield at harvest time? One thing he did know. He needed to pray a lot, because so much was at stake.

Making it in Central Falls High School:
Guillermo Ronquillo (left) and Bryant Estrada (right).

Appendix 1
Guillermo's College Essay

I believe that some human beings are born with a certain competitive edge that nature has proven vital for survival. When in the face of defeat, this competitive nature removes all that is base in our beings, and brings out what is necessary to achieve victory in our everyday struggles. In my life, it is not a battle or a struggle for survival in nature which brings out the best in me, but rather a struggle for success. Furthermore, it is this competitive nature that allows me to fight and overcome all that stands in my way.

So what happens to those who choose to give up rather than pursue their goals? I suppose they are merely too afraid of failure to even try to be successful. I do not believe that a person is a coward if they feel fear, but once that person allows fear to overcome their sense of duty, they become one. My duty is to my God and to my family first. They have always protected and supported me. My duty is to love them and to honor them in everything I do.

Secondly, I have a duty to one day be happy and successful. In every step of my life I have never let go of that sense of duty. That is why every night before I go to bed and every morning before I go to school, I kneel down before my God and ask him for his guidance and for strength. My dreams and goals are driven by that very sense of duty, and my competitive nature compels me to do the best that I can do. These two qualities, duty and competitiveness, are deep within my character, and they only grow stronger as I overcome obstacles in my daily life.

At the age of nine, my move from El Salvador to the United States presented a series of challenges. There was a stark contrast between my academic abilities in the two countries. Not only did I confront a significant communication barrier due to my limited English skills, but also the system of education to which I was subjected left me confused. Nevertheless, my competitive nature and developing motivation to surmount obstacles met these challenges head on. Ironically, it was the drastic change in grades and proficiency that has compelled me to reach the top of my high school class today.

During my first year in the ESL class, my teacher was trying to explain to me how in English, as opposed to Spanish, an adjective can come before a noun. When she saw that I was having a hard time, she got up to leave and said "stupid kid" under her breath. Though I didn't speak English, I knew exactly what she had said. The single incident awoke my competitive nature and made me work harder. One year later, I was moved into mainstream English classes. Because of my inherent desire to advance and the support I found in other teachers, I was able to adapt.

I learned two valuable things from my move to the United States. One is that, though there will always be naysayers, there are even more people who believe in me. In the face of defeat, they plant enough hope in my mind and heart to keep me moving forward. Secondly, I learned that, while my environment changed completely, this country has provided fertile ground for me to grow as a better person, a hardworking student, and ultimately, a success.

Charles Darwin said that the organism that is most likely to survive is that which is capable of adapting to a new environment. This notion not only applies to the scientific world, but also in the human race towards success. The environments in which we live, work, and study will change. The survivors are those who learn to adapt. In my academic career, after adopting a new culture, I learned to adapt as the social and educational conditions changed. These conditions change for all students as they move on to each subsequent grade level.

Some will give up, while others, the survivors, will advance. I am a survivor. My past experiences have proven so. Moving on to college, and later on to medical school, the challenges will only heighten. Whether it is trying to find a way to pay for college tuition, or struggling through an exam, I know the path I have chosen is not an easy one. Even so, driven by my competitiveness and my duties, and keeping my faith in God, I will be successful. For those who believe in me, I will work hard. In the face of naysayers, I will work even harder to prove them wrong.

MONOPOLY: SURREAL BECOMING REALITY

I went down to the basement to help my mother clean out some old stuff; she said that the cleaning was "a time to throw away the useless junk that had been building up over the years." I searched through my childhood toys, different things that I had not seen for many years. A Monopoly box was at the bottom of the pile; it was a game that I had not seen or played since I was ten, when I would wake up on Saturdays at seven o'clock in the morning to watch cartoons and play with my older sister. As I opened the dusty box, many childhood memories came running through my head. The game board fell to the floor and it opened, I rolled the dice; the game had begun.

The board began to tremble on the ground. Everything disappeared and the world around me seemed to turn back. A sudden light began to envelop my surroundings, and I noticed I was no longer in the basement with my childhood memorabilia. Everything looked very similar, as if I had seen it all before, I was on the game board! Two dice fell onto the floor and my body unwillingly began to move. It was as if the dice was controlling me and was leading me through the game.

Every time the dice rolled, I landed on different spaces that entitled me to buy property or houses, and go to jail. Every space that I moved to seemed to have a correlation to my different life experiences. When I landed on the Boardwalk, I was given the chance to buy a property on that space, which symbolized the opportunities I have had by joining college access programs like the Upward Bound and the College

Crusade of Rhode Island. Just like buying properties helped me win the game, these programs have helped me succeed in high school.

I am proud to be the valedictorian of my senior class and leader in my community. Additionally, sometimes landing on "Chance" meant that I had to "Go to Jail." To me, "Going to Jail" signified the obstacles or struggles I have encountered in my life, which I consider to be fate or chance because I was not able to have control over them, like struggling to become valedictorian or trying to be a successful individual coming from an underprivileged city. These among other things, including the death of my grandfather, were all the challenges I had to face during my high school career. On the one hand, the accomplishments I obtained, I consider them personal choice and will because they have allowed me to excel in life.

As I proceeded through the spaces on the game board, I was amazed to see such a strong connection between my life and a common childhood board game. Suddenly, I heard a trembling noise coming from underneath the game, everything began to shake and the board split into two as if there were some sort of earthquake. I fell through the crevice, and my surroundings disappeared. I heard the familiar voice of my mother calling down to me; I opened my eyes and noticed that I was no longer on the board but back in the basement with the dice at hand and the broken board on the floor. At that time, it became evident that the dream was no longer surreal; it was reality.

Resources

Alliance for Excellent Education Fact Sheet, "Latino Students and U.S. High Schools." Washington D.C., January 2009. www.all4ed.org/files/Latino_FactSheet.pdf.

Balfanz, Robert, and Nellie Legters. "Locating the Dropout Crisis." Baltimore, MD: Center for Research on the Education of Students Placed at Risk, Johns Hopkins University, September 2004.

———. "The Graduation Rate Crisis We Know and What Can Be Done About It." *Education Week* commentary (July 12, 2006).

Borg, Linda. "Central Falls High Gets a Makeover." *Providence Journal* (July 21, 2009).

Bradley, Ann. "High Schools: No Quick Fixes." EPE Research Center: Education Counts, June 8, 2007. www.edcounts.org/archive/sreports/qc98/solutions/so-n2.htm.

Children's Defense Fund. "Cradle to Prison Pipeline Fact Sheet, Rhode Island," March 2009. www.childrensdefense.org/child-research-data-publications/data/state-data-repository/cradle-to-prison-pipeline/cradle-prison-pipeline-rhode-island-2009-fact-sheet.pdf.

Education Trust. "Latino Achievement in America." Washington, D.C., 2003. www.theadvocatesforhumanrights.org/sites/608a3887-dd53-4796-8904-997a0131ca54/uploads/LatAchievEnglish_2.pdf.

Fry, Richard. "The Changing Pathways of Hispanic Youths Into Adulthood." Pew Hispanic Center, Washington, D.C., October 2009. pewhispanic.org/reports/report.php?ReportID=114.

———. "Latinos in Higher Education: Many Enroll, Too Few Graduate." Pew Hispanic Center, Washington, D.C., 2002. www.eric.ed.gov:80/ERICDocs/data/ericdocs2sql/content_storage_01/0000019b/80/1a/69/b4.pdf.

Gist, Deborah. "Protocol for Interventions: Persistently Lowest Achieving Schools." Rhode Island Department of Education, January 2010. www.ride .ri.gov/ride/Docs/Protocol_for_Interventions.pdf.

Gross, Terry, Executive Director. Institute for Study and Practice of Non-violence. Narrative written to Public Safety Grant Administration, State of Rhode Island, 2007.

Griggs, Shirley, and Rita Dunn. "Hispanic-American Students and Learning Style." *ERIC Digest*: ED 393607, Urbana, Illinois, 1996.

"Hunger and Homelessness Increase in American Cities." A Report by the U.S. Conference of Mayors, December 2008.

Information Works, Rhode Island Department of Education, 2007–2009. www.infoworks.ride.uri.edu/2009/default.asp.

Lopez, Mark. "Latinos and Education: Explaining the Attainment Gap." Pew Hispanic Center, Washington, D.C., October 2009. pewhispanic.org/reports/ report.php?ReportID=115.

Maeroff, Gene. *Altered Destinies: Making Life Better for Schoolchildren in Need*. New York: Palgrave MacMillan, 1999.

———. *Building Blocks: Making Children Successful in the Early Years of School*. New York: Palgrave MacMillan, 2006.

Middleton, Diana. "Landing a Job of the Future Takes a Two-Track Mind." *The Wall Street Journal* (December 29, 2009).

Office of Minority Health, "Latino/Hispanic American Culture and Health." Rhode Island Department of Health, April 2009. www.health.ri.gov/chic/ minority/office.php.

Padron, Yolanda, et al. "Educating Hispanic Students: Obstacles and Avenues to Improve Education." Center for Research in Education, Diversity and Excellence, University of Houston, 2002.

Patinkin, Mark. "Dropout Tales of Hardship, Hope." *Providence Journal* (June 10, 2008).

Portillo, Zortillo. "Latin America Gets Poor Marks." Review of a study by the Inter-American Development Bank (IDB) on the poor quality of Latin American public education, March 1999.

Report of the commissioner's visit to Central Falls High School, Rhode Island Department of Education, April 2007.

Report of the visiting committee, "Central Falls High School," New England Association of Schools and Colleges, Commission on Public Secondary Schools, April 2002.

Research data on immigration compiled by Pew Hispanic Center, Washington, D.C., 2007–2009.

Rhode Island *KIDS COUNT.* "Indicators of Child Well-Being, Profile of Central Falls, Rhode Island," April 2009. www.rikidscount.org/matriarch/documents/Central%20Falls2009%281%29.pdf.

Rotella, Carlo. "Class Warrior." *The New Yorker* (February 10, 2010): A profile of Arne Duncan.

Schrader, Esther. Review of *Strangers Among Us: How Latino Immigration Is Transforming America* by Robert Suro. *Washington Monthly* (October 1998).

UCLA Civil Rights Project. "Report from Civil Rights Project Shows Racial Inequality Growing in America's Schools." *UCLA News* (September 2007).

U.S. Department of Education, National Center for Educational Statistics. "The Condition of Education." Washington, D.C., 2006.

Ziner, Karen. "Some Immigrants Are Afraid to Give Information to the Government." *Providence Sunday Journal* (November 8, 2009).

About the Author

William R. Holland is a former secondary school teacher and administrator, school superintendent of four school districts, and executive director of the Rhode Island Principals Association and is professor emeritus of educational leadership at Rhode Island College. He also served as Rhode Island Commissioner of Education from 1999 to 2002 and interim superintendent of Central Falls School District during the 2006–2007 school year.

Dr. Holland is the author of two books on educational leadership and has just completed a crime book. He and his wife live in Narragansett, Rhode Island, and have three grown children and seven grandchildren who happily occupy a great deal of their time.